THE SEARCH FOR SELF AND
THE SEARCH FOR GOD

Daphne
Publications

Also by Bud Harris, Ph.D.

Cracking Open: A Memoir of Struggling, Passages, and Transformations

Sacred Selfishness: A Guide to Living a Life of Substance

The Father Quest: Rediscovering an Elemental Force

Resurrecting the Unicorn: Masculinity in the 21st Century

The Fire and the Rose: The Wedding of Spirituality and Sexuality

Knowing the Questions Living the Answers: A Jungian Guide Through the Paradoxes of Peace, Conflict and Love that Mark a Lifetime

Coauthored with Massimilla Harris, Ph.D.:

Into the Heart of the Feminine: An Archetypal Journey to Renew Strength, Love, and Creativity

Like Gold Through Fire: Understanding the Transforming Power of Suffering

The Art of Love: The Craft of Relationships: A Practical Guide for Creating the Loving Relationships We Want

THE SEARCH
FOR SELF

and

THE SEARCH
FOR GOD

Three Jungian Lectures and Seminars
to Guide the Journey

BUD HARRIS, PH.D.
Jungian Analyst

DAPHNE PUBLICATIONS • ASHEVILLE, NORTH CAROLINA

THE SEARCH FOR SELF AND THE SEARCH FOR GOD:
THREE JUNGIAN LECTURES AND SEMINARS TO GUIDE THE JOURNEY
COPYRIGHT © 2015 BY BUD HARRIS, PH.D.

DAPHNE PUBLICATIONS, AN IMPRINT OF SPES, INC.

Harris, Clifton T. Bud
The search for self and the search for god: three jungian lectures and seminars to guide the journey / Bud Harris

ISBN 978-0-692-47671-0   Non-fiction
1. Psychology 2. Jungian psychology 3. Spirituality

Cover Design by Courtney Tiberio
Interior Layout by Susan Yost

Author's Note:
This book comprises the text of three lectures and the seminars that accompanied them.

I have presented these lectures and seminars in Asheville, North Carolina, and in many other cities in the United States over the last ten years. The book includes the questions I asked to spark the audience's reflections and participation. I have included the exercises from the seminars as well, with the hope that you will find them stimulating and useful. As much as possible, I have maintained the original text of each lecture as it was delivered. I believe this makes the lectures more personal and easier to read and doesn't risk changing any of my implied or intended meaning.

Contents

Introduction   *ix*

PART ONE
Sacred Selfishness: The Path to Love and Authenticity   1

Chapter 1 : Lecture   3

Chapter 2 : Seminar   21

PART TWO
**Fire in the Soul: A Jungian Guide to Discovering the
Promise in Our Holy Longing**   45

Chapter 3 : Lecture   47

Chapter 4 : Seminar   71

PART THREE
**Becoming Whole as a Spiritual Necessity: A Jungian Guide
for Renewing the Mystic Vision**   93

Chapter 5 : Lecture   95

Chapter 6 : Seminar   121

Resources   143

Introduction

In my memoir *Cracking Open: A Memoir of Struggling, Passages, and Transformation*, I shared very personal reflections about the intersection of two transformational periods in my life. In particular, I told the story of how I felt betrayed by my God and my religion during a traumatic period in my childhood. Also in *Cracking Open*, I recounted how, after being furious with God for a few decades, I found myself in Zurich, Switzerland, training to become a Jungian analyst and, as part of the training, in analysis with Dr. John Mattern, a gifted analyst and extraordinary human being. During one of our afternoon sessions, John quietly remarked to me that anyone who was as mad with God as I was, must be in for a lifelong spiritual quest. I left that session—mad at John for even suggesting that—and I pensively walked out into the park by Lake Zurich…still fuming.

But as the weeks went by, I began to realize that John might be right. Also, at that same time, I was beginning to prepare for my upcoming exam in Comparative Religions at the Jung Institute. As a background for these exams, I had to write a paper and I chose to compare the Lakota vision quest, the steps in the mystical journey of the great mystics in the Middle Ages, and C. G. Jung's individuation process. In researching the paper and preparing for the exam, I began to recognize the depths of my spiritual longings and my desire for a path that would satisfy them.

Both these longings that I felt—and the path that I have discovered and developed—unfold in this book. My intention in sharing this material is not to convince anyone of any kind of religious truth. My goal is simply to share my thoughts and journey, and to hope that, in some way, you will find them useful.

Early in my work in Zurich, I learned that the God I hated in my memoir, *Cracking Open*, and was furious with for decades, was, in reality, the image of God that I had been indoctrinated into having during my childhood. Now in my perspective, the word God has become a metaphor for the great mystery of life and the creative, purposeful, directing energy of the Self that contains my inherent potentials, and guides and affects my life from within, and—through my responses to events and synchronicities—forms it, from without. For me, today, my image of God has to be a creative one that evolves as I evolve, while at the same time, it is fueling my journey into wholeness, holiness—my individuation.

It is clear to me that since childhood, God—or in reality, my current image of God—has always been a personal issue. Based on my experiences and history, I continue to need an image that I can relate to personally, that I can grapple with and be inspired by—that can grow, and transform, and push my growth. Conceptual terms like the "Divine," my "Higher Power," or the "Transcendent" don't sufficiently engage me personally. I don't mean for anyone else to adopt my perspective, and I'm okay with your developing the images of the great mystery that are meaningful to you. So please keep this in mind as you read this book.

In Zurich, I became keenly aware of the power of the deep, innate, substrate patterns within us, which are called archetypes. In particular, I came to understand that religion and spirituality are the great, primordial archetypal pathways that offer the possibility of connecting to the Self, to God within us. Through these universal pathways of religion and spirituality, we can find, if we search deep within ourselves, an archetypal, living myth that can nurture, inspire, and sustain us and give perspective and meaning to our lives. Yet, this living, sacred principle must also be able to evolve in our psyche or soul, as we ourselves evolve throughout our lives. It must be able to continue to support our connection to the Self, God within us (or, if you would prefer, the Divine or Transcendent Presence within us). Our spiritual selves actually need these ongoing, religious/spiritual practices and recognitions, that can, in a day-to-day way, support and inspire our connection to, and our love of, life and the presence of the Self and the Divine within us.

An aspect of our spiritual quest is to become whole, to become fully human. Becoming fully human ultimately means recognizing with awe and fear, the presence of the Self within us—how it has, and is, operating within our lives, challenging us to grow in a way that fulfills its pattern for us—challenging us to be fully engaged in life, and to be creative in our vision of life. It also includes "slamming" us against the walls of failure, humiliation, and illness, when we refuse to acknowledge it. These powerful human primal principles—religion and spirituality—are indeed "a call" and the implications of this reality seem to escape most of us. If our self-awareness begins to grow, even a little bit, we soon see that ignoring the presence of these powerful "calls" means they will be "lived out" through our shadows, sublimated into achievement, materialism, and addictions, or require so much energy to keep repressed that our psyches and bodies will lose their vitality.

From my book, *Cracking Open* and the contents of this book, I think that it becomes clear that individuation has required me to become liberated from the person that I had been shaped, formed, and indoctrinated into being, as I grew up. This liberation, through developing self-awareness, has been and is the foundation for my growing consciousness and for becoming real. I have devoted my book, *Sacred Selfishness: Living a Life of Substance* to the specifics of this process.

Transformation and individuation are not the result of our intellectual activities. They are the products of our experiences that have become consciously known, and are used to change who we are and how we live. True self-knowledge brings transformation. What we think of as the self-knowledge that comes naturally with age, but is not consciously rooted in the willingness to continually pursue transformation, does little to add to either our consciousness or our wholeness. The development of fruitful self-knowledge calls us into a continuing confrontation with ourselves and our experiences.

There is a common thread that runs throughout these lectures and seminars. Professionally, it is called individuation. Personally, I call it the search for Self and the search for God. However one designates it, individuation is a path of awakening, transforming, becoming conscious, fully engaged in living, being authentically alive, and fulfilling the unique pattern within ourselves.

In Part One, "Sacred Selfishness: A Guide for Cultivating a Life of Love, Authenticity, and Substance," we are reminded that in his "Zarathustra" seminar, Jung affirmed that we must eat the gold of the world until we are made of gold, and not of hunger.

In Chapter 1, Sacred Selfishness is the path of filling ourselves with gold. This path is based on the classical quest stories that reveal the journey to personal consciousness and help us examine all our assumptions about ourselves and our lives, to assist us in uncovering our hidden potentials. This chapter explains how I developed the idea of Sacred Selfishness in the context of Jung's theory of individuation. The chapter also provides an overview of how this path unfolds theoretically and in everyday life, and of how real love grows from the foundation of self-love.

In Chapter 2, we will explore the directives most of us are taught from childhood—that we are supposed to be generous, to give to others, and to meet the needs of people around us. We will see how Jung's insistence that we eat the gold of the world and accumulate psychological abundance differs from these early teachings and opposes society's demands that we achieve predetermined goals in order to feel successful and worthwhile. We will learn that our early lessons and society's values leave us with unmet, often hidden, needs and desires, especially those for love, passion, and authenticity. As we seek to understand the personal and collective influences that have molded our lives and created our scripts, we will discover the ways we can free ourselves from these influences, thus allowing the potentials we have formerly curtailed to flourish with new life and to transform us.

In Part Two, "Fire in the Soul: A Jungian Guide to Discovering the Promise in Our Holy Longing," we will see that to be human is to be filled with longing. Even if we have achieved good lives, we still seem to long for safety, health, love, family, peace, abundance, and freedom from anxiety. Beneath the busy, and often frantic, imagined importance of our lives, we long to be assured that our lives have purpose and meaning, that our perception of reality is true, and that we have value to something greater than ourselves.

Chapter 3 will focus on the spirit of individuation in Jungian psychology by exploring how it may become a guide to reawakening and re-imagining the archetypal and mythic dimensions of our spiritual and religious depths. We will ask ourselves, "What is religion?" and how do the institutional, the personal, and the psychological differ? We will also examine how spirituality and religion are different, yet both flow from within us. Then we will explore how Jungian psychology can help us let go of the pressure to "believe" and approach the religious function in our psyche with integrity. This path can enliven our traditions if we so choose, while it becomes the foundation for taking responsibility for our own spiritual path in a way that is truly transforming and enlightening.

Chapter 4 will continue to lead us into a more profound vision of the spiritual dimensions of the individuation process. In this journey, the idea is not just to love yourself, but how to give love to yourself. The idea is not how to be good, but how to live with purpose and meaning. The idea is not just how to heal your suffering and your past, but how to be transformed by them. And the idea is not just how to make life Holy; it is how to become co-creators of yourself and the world with the Self and the Divine with you. This journey will follow a tapestry of mythological images, stories, and psychological realities that will guide our search into our religious and spiritual potentials in order to discover how these potentials can transform and enrich our lives.

Part Three, "Becoming Whole as a Spiritual Necessity: A Jungian Guide for Renewing the Mystic Vision" will examine the importance of the mystic vision to all our lives. In his last great book, *Mysterium Conjunctionis*, Jung points out that it is the mystic vision that takes us out of religious decay. The mystics carry the Soul Force of religion. They bear the mystery that can return creativity to religion and transform it into a spiritual quest emanating from the ground of our being. When the Soul Force is lost, religious institutions become fear-based and leave many of us feeling wounded and alienated.

In Chapter 5, we will carefully study how Jung's emphasis on the spiritual life as a journey toward wholeness heals these wounds, supports, and guides personal spiritual development, and offers a new vision of renewal to our institutions.

In Chapter 6, we will see that renewing the mystic vision is more than an intellectual exercise. The mystic vision's paths and practices engage us fully in life and, through growing self-knowledge, soften and strengthen us while helping us to love life and other people. The process of becoming whole, the individuation process, becomes a spiritual necessity when we recognize the dynamic, creative emphasis on transformation—our true spiritual quest is to become fully human and fully alive. We will explore how we are challenged individually to revitalize the Soul Force in our lives and how Jungian psychology offers us a modern path to restore that vision. Individuation and the mystic vision emphasize that mind, body, and spirit are connected by the level of consciousness we grow into, and this kind of growth is the path of love and individuation.

The material that I deal with in these lectures has grown from the experiences of my life—experiences that I am very thankful for. Of course developing this material has transformed me in more ways than I can explain. I believe that all our efforts to examine who we are and where we are going in order to heal ourselves and our culture are sacred activities. I hope that you will join me in this work with that same spirit. I must also add that presenting this material and interacting with audiences around the country also transformed me significantly and left me deeply moved by the potentials in the human spirit.

PART ONE

SACRED SELFISHNESS:
The Path to Love and Authenticity

"If you fulfill the pattern that is peculiar to yourself, you have loved yourself, you have accumulated and have abundance; you bestow virtue then because you have luster. You radiate; from your abundance something overflows. But if you hate and despise yourself—if you have not accepted your pattern—then there are hungry animals (prowling cats and other beasts and vermin) in your constitution which get at your neighbors like flies in order to satisfy the appetites which you have failed to satisfy."

– C. G. JUNG, *NIETZSCHE'S ZARATHUSTRA*, VOL. 2, P. 801

"I have frequently seen people become neurotic when they content themselves with inadequate or wrong answers to the questions of life. They seek position, marriage, reputation, outward success or money, and remain unhappy and neurotic even when they have attained what they were seeking. Such people are usually confined within too narrow a spiritual horizon. Their life has not sufficient meaning. If they are enabled to develop more spacious personalities, the neurosis generally disappears. For that reason the idea of development was always of the highest importance to me."

– C. G. JUNG, *MEMORIES, DREAMS, REFLECTIONS*, P. 140

Chapter 1 : Lecture

SACRED SELFISHNESS:
The Path to Love and Authenticity

When I think back about the southern culture that I was raised in, I remember very clearly being told, "Don't be selfish," again and again. Before too long, whenever the word *selfish* was mentioned, I immediately thought of the Golden Rule or that I should be devoting myself to loving my neighbor. These responses had become conditioned in me in stronger ways than Pavlov could have dreamed of. And then, somewhere around midlife, I faintly began to hear the idea that if you don't or can't love yourself, what you do for your neighbor may not turn out to be all that great. That idea left me in a quandary. So, I want to begin by amplifying that quandary. And in order to do that, I am going to ask you three questions.

Now, I don't want you to answer them yet. I just want you to keep them in mind and see how your responses to them may evolve. And I want you to see how keeping them in mind will change you. These questions come up whenever we make choices.

1. Will this decision contribute to my self-love?
2. Will this decision contribute to my individuation process—my process of authentic growth and development?
3. What do you think of the ethics and morality of the first two questions? Are these questions a sign of being good or bad, selfish or unselfish, profound, or what?

3

Fulfilling Your Individual Pattern

Now, as I hope you can imagine, I've had a lot of fun with the title *Sacred Selfishness*. Most people love it. But there are a few who are scandalized by it. These people have trouble understanding that I have defined *sacred selfishness* in a way that represents the opposite pole of how we usually think of selfishness. Sacred selfishness means making the commitment to valuing ourselves and our lives enough to become people of substance, people who are filled with gold—who aren't hollow or filled with lead. It's a commitment to building the foundation that will support our growing capacity to give and receive love.

It was actually Nietzsche's use of the term *sickly selfishness* that inspired my title *Sacred Selfishness*. In everyday life, we generally think of sickly selfishness as egotism or individualism. Its practitioners are emotionally hungry for power, starved for affirmation, and driven to use and impose on us for self-serving ends. Narcissism is like sickly selfishness. It is self-infatuation, an obsession that actually reflects an inability to love oneself or anyone else.

In considering these ideas, I was particularly inspired by some of Jung's comments in the second volume of his *Zarathustra* seminars. Let me share a few words from Jung to give you the flavor of them. He said,

> If you fulfill the pattern that is peculiar to yourself, you have loved yourself, you have accumulated and have abundance; you bestow virtue then because you have luster. You radiate; from your abundance something overflows. But if you hate and despise yourself—if you have not accepted your pattern—then there are hungry animals (prowling cats and other beasts and vermin) in your constitution which get at your neighbors like flies in order to satisfy the appetites which you have failed to satisfy. Therefore, Nietzsche says to those people who have not fulfilled their individual pattern that the bestowing soul is lacking. There is no radiation, no real warmth; there is hunger and secret stealing.

Jung is reminding us that if we have been fulfilling the Divine pattern within us, we will have an abundance of heart and soul. We will

4

inspire and empower the people we come in contact with. But if we have refused this inner quest, even though it may appear we are saying and doing the right thing, we will leave people who come in contact with us feeling diminished.

When Jung speaks about the pattern that is peculiar to oneself, he is speaking about the path of individuation, which he explains as "the process by which individuals are formed and differentiated; in the particular, it is the development of the psychological individual as being distinct from the general collective psychology." This process becomes life at its fullest when it is based upon *personal awareness*.

As we learn to read our experiences and understand their depths, our growing self-knowledge is reflected in our choices of values and actions. Now, I'm sure most of you already know this. What we have to keep in mind is that the whole point of individuation is that the *world* needs people who have come alive, who live from the heart, who embrace risk and struggle to live, whose lives are a sacred task in which *holiness* is passion and the way to the *Divine* is through the pursuit of self-knowledge.

Jung's words in his *Zarathustra* lectures helped me understand that individuation is a journey into loving oneself and loving life. My intention has been to write a road map for this journey. In his more relaxed seminars, such as the one on *Zarathustra*, Jung had no problem mixing psychology and religion. Jung realized that the roles of psychology and religion are to help provide the infrastructure within us to support our growth and our search for meaning in order to give us the ability to live by our values and to love. Jung was completely aware of the spiritual question being asked of religion by the human heart of modern people.

Martin Buber articulated this question for us as follows: "Can you teach me to have faith in reality, in the truth of our existence, so that my life will have purpose, meaning, and a way of being fulfilled?" That was exactly the question I needed to face when my life was floundering so badly at the age of thirty-three—the story I share in my book *Sacred Selfishness*. But at the time, I didn't have a clue about what I really needed, and it took me quite a journey to simply discover the questions.

Jung had become aware of the spiritual search for love and meaning early in his work. His *Zarathustra* seminars took place before my birth. The experience Jung had with the people who came to see him professionally (and, by the way, my experience is much the same) suggests that institutionalized religion—and I would add institutionalized psychology—was not that helpful in their search for love and meaning. As many of you know, Jung went on to conclude—and he made this observation to a convention of pastors in 1932—that every serious problem that his patients encountered in the second half of life is a spiritual problem and results from the lack of a spiritual orientation toward life.

Now I found that an absolutely amazing statement the first time I read it. I understand this statement as saying that our anxiety, depression, weight problems, sexual problems, addictions, and so on all represent the lack of a spiritual orientation toward life once we have established a workable identity or, in our professional language, a relatively strong ego. In order to truly understand Jung's statement, we need to understand how he visualized human growth and development. As most of you know, we use the development of consciousness as a guide for understanding our spiritual and psychological growth. Jung, as I have said, calls this process individuation. Interestingly, Evelyn Underhill, the great Anglican scholar on mysticism, also considers the mystical path as the development of consciousness, although she calls it the development of spiritual consciousness.

Simple Consciousness

Even though consciousness may always be evolving, I use a simplified illustration in the book *Sacred Selfishness,* outlining it in four stages. The first stage I write about is called *simple consciousness,* which encompasses the naïve, developing consciousness of childhood. This period of development begins with birth and includes the years of our early lives, when our potential to learn and act responsibly is being developed. Our parents, families, schools, churches, places in society, and the media introduce us to life in the world.

Complex Consciousness

As we grow through adolescence and into adulthood, we enter stage 2:

complex consciousness. Psychologically, growth is a time of action and activities by which we are learning to fulfill the societal tasks of adulthood. First we must learn to function in society—especially in terms of work and relationships. And in order to accomplish these tasks, we must develop an identity—in technical terms, an ego and a workable persona.

It is important to keep in mind that our identity is based on what we identify with or put ourselves in opposition to. In healing problems in our development, analysts and therapists generally utilize empathy, mirroring, understanding, insight, problem solving, and a focus on childhood and adolescence. The purpose of these approaches is to rebuild the inner ground that supports our identity and ability to love and work. In our consulting rooms today, we often encounter men and women who are stuck between simple consciousness and complex consciousness—unable to make it into full adulthood, unable to become self-responsible and effective as members of society. The Jungian analyst Erich Neumann, in *The Origins and History of Consciousness*, refers to these people as "strugglers," and they challenge us professionally to know more about developmental or ego psychology.

Most of us must be well into the stage of complex consciousness before we can understand Jung's statement about our problems being based on the lack of a religious or spiritual attitude. Complex consciousness is also the stage we refer to as normal adulthood.

Individual Consciousness

In my experience, the most difficult point in our growth is the transformational movement from complex consciousness, normal adulthood, into stage 3: the more personally authentic stage of *individual consciousness.* I think a great deal of this difficulty is the result of our culture's need to idolize identity. In our media-based society, identity rests on recognition and power and emphasizes controlling the impression we make on other people, even when they are the ones we love and are closest to. One of the greatest inhibitions triggered by this transition is the fear that others will believe we have lost control of our lives, have forsaken time-honored values, and are behaving in ways that are selfish or odd.

In his book, Erich Neumann describes society's influence on our growth and development as the power of the "world parents." He emphasizes that we must first differentiate from the effects of our personal parents and then from the effects of the world parents. I believe, particularly in recent years, we Jungians haven't paid nearly enough attention to understanding society's influence on us. We slipped into the assumption that in many cases, analysis or therapy will automatically take care of these influences.

The psychoanalyst Erich Fromm has been very articulate in his explanation of how our society molds us. I want to pay attention to what he describes as the social character, because it determines what people think of as normal. This means the social character influences many, if not most, of the things we worry about and experience in everyday life. I myself find that the demands and values of our social character also show up to haunt me, to cause conflicts and struggles with shame and guilt in almost every transformation that I go through.

Fromm defines social character by saying that every society develops an image of the "model person" needed to keep its values and institutions operating. In turn, society's institutions—such as the family, schools, churches, the media, and advertising—attempt to mold our development into a personality that fits the model of our society's social character. Therefore, the social character of our culture provides the fundamental traits we identify with and becomes the foundation of our identity, as well as the definition of what is normal.

Over the years I've become very interested in Erich Fromm's work. He was a psychoanalyst, also trained as a rabbi, who analyzed the nature of Western society. Over thirty-five years ago, he said that we live in a consumer-driven, marketing culture that emphasizes competition, success, self-sufficiency, individualism, and material progress. He concluded that in general, (1) our self-worth rests on achievements and possessions and (2) and the true Golden Rule of our society is to consume.

This means that happiness rests on having "more": If we feel unhappy or bad, we consume to feel better. We go shopping, eat more, drink more, and even consume relationships, medications, and so on. In other words, the forces of the culture shape our personality in such a

8

way that we want to do what we must do for society to function along its current values. Social necessities are transformed into personal needs.

Fromm wrote a wonderful essay that you don't even need to read because his title says it all. The title is "The Psychopathology of Normalcy." I think that it's easy to see where he's coming from. Jung, like most of the great theorists in depth psychology, agrees with this point. It can be summed up by saying that what we think of as normal is in fact one-sided, indifferent to the personal or individual aspects of life, unfeeling, and incapable of true psychological and spiritual development. In other words, normal is always pathological because it's always split off from the real person.

As analysts and therapists, the reality that normal is always pathological often places us in a difficult paradox. For example, I open my book *Sacred Selfishness* with the story of a woman who comes into my office and tells me she is exhausted. She then goes on to tell me how hard she has worked on her marriage, how much counseling she and her husband have been to, and how hard she has tried to be a good mother. Finally she collapses in tears and exclaims, "I just want to be normal and happy."

Every time I hear this plaintive lament, I am touched by how very human it is to "just want to be normal and happy." But wanting to be normal, which appears deceptively peaceful, leaves us preferring not to look into our unconscious or our dreams, because we are afraid we will discover weird, scary, and shameful aspects of ourselves that we have repressed in order to fit in. In fact, what we have really repressed is our ability to see reality truthfully, our authentic personhood, our emotional relationship to life, our creativity, and our ability to grow and become. Many of our childhood wounds revolve around situations where we felt shamed or discouraged or inadequate or embarrassed or we didn't live up to our family's or teacher's expectations—the whole circle of effects that emanate from the influence of the social demands in our society. The attitudes and values of the social character are actually so insidious that they are basically unconscious to most of us. We're not aware that these are the values that we're incorporating into our personality and that we are living by.

It is helpful to keep in mind that conventional or normal reality is always a fiction. All of the great mystical traditions as well as depth psychology consider it an illusion. Both psychological development and spiritual development rest on separating ourselves from these fictions.

As mentioned, from the stage of complex consciousness, we then grow into the next stage, individual consciousness. This stage begins when we are able to become increasingly aware of ourselves as separate from the forces that molded us, when the knowledge of our shadow begins to shake the foundation of the values and characteristics that we identified with in order to form our identities. This stage too begins as a time of action, as we seek help to gain new strength and vitality by seeking insight and self-knowledge.

Generally, we begin this stage by trying to understand our shadow and our humanity. In *Sacred Selfishness*, I refer to Carl Rogers as a man who has achieved this kind of self-knowledge. Dr. Rogers, one of the founders of humanistic psychology, addressed a group of physicians in their residency training that was attended by Dr. Rachel Naomi Remen. She reports that before giving a clinical demonstration, Carl Rogers said the following:

> Before every session I take a moment to remember my humanity…There is no experience that this man has that I cannot share with him, no fear that I cannot understand, no suffering that I cannot care about, because I too am human. No matter how deep his wound, he does not need to be ashamed in front of me. I too am vulnerable. And because of this, I am enough. Whatever his story, he no longer needs to be alone with it. This is what will allow his healing to begin.

Discovery of Fierceness

Inherent in this quest is the discovery of our fierceness, the valuing of our bodies and our instinctual nature. As the door opens to personal authenticity, we learn to be kind when kindness is appropriate and aggressive when it is required. Let me repeat that: We learn to be kind

10

when kindness is appropriate and aggressive when it is required. Being fierce is something that many of us were not brought up to be very comfortable with.

There is an old story of Saint Francis and the wolf that has helped me develop a sense of comfort, even affection with the savage side of myself. The story takes place a long time ago when there were still vast forests in Italy. The people in a small village began to notice that some of their chickens and livestock were disappearing. Soon, an occasional child or older person would be missing. As the villagers put together a few clues—bloody bits of fur, signs of struggles, and paw prints—they realized a ferocious wolf had moved into the nearby woods.

While animals and weaker people were customary prey, the wolf seemed to be getting increasingly bolder. The villagers tried in vain to poison, capture, or kill the wolf, but were unable to even find it. They called for hunters from near and far to hunt it. Elegant nobles with great horses, packs of hounds, and many retainers tried to help the villagers. But the wolf evaded them all.

Eventually the village elders, in desperation, sent a message to Saint Francis. Saint Francis came immediately to their aid. He arrived at the village and plunged into the forest, without pausing to eat or rest. He journeyed deeper into the dense vegetation than anyone had before, searching for the wolf's lair. In the twilight of a small clearing, he found the wolf. They stood before each other, eye to eye, for some time. Finally, Saint Francis said simply, "Brother wolf."

When Saint Francis returned to the village, the excited people gathered around him and begged him to tell them how to deal with the wolf. He said to them, "Feed your wolf." The lesson is simple. We must face our capacity for fierceness. Feeding it means honoring it with conscious awareness and integrating it into our personalities as part of our journey into wholeness. Feeding our wolf is necessary to give us the strength not only to support a life of love and responsibility and but also to respond to personal and social problems with caring and competence—responses that honor our tradition of human dignity, the sacredness of each person, and our ideal of a community in which people help each other.

Questions to Expand Our Understanding

1. As I have talked about individuation, Martin Buber's questions about meaning and fulfillment, the culture's influence on our identity, and finally our shadows, what kinds of images, memories, thoughts, feelings, or questions have come up for you?

2. Do you have any additional comments on Erich Fromm's idea of the psychopathology of normalcy?

3. Feeding our fierceness—how do we do that? This is always an important question.

4. What are some of our defenses against our fierceness, which might also include our passion?

Developing Individual Consciousness

There are two particular problems that most of us encounter when we are trying to grow out of normal adulthood into individual consciousness. The first of these is a feeling of loneliness. Whenever we begin to change, it is not unusual for our spouses, partners, children, and friends to work hard at trying to revive the person we used to be—the person they recall with love and respect, the person they thought they could understand and even control in many cases, or the person they could at least depend upon not to make them face new challenges. I've found that those close to us will often go as far as to accuse us of being arrogant, self-centered, and irresponsible as we press onward toward self-growth. These responses add to the pain of our transformations. But they also teach us that part of what we must give up is the approval—the very approval that pleased us as children—we get from others by meeting their needs and expectations.

I can still remember an event that happened over sixty years ago. I was about six years old and was sitting on the floor, playing with my little cars and trucks. After a few minutes, my three-year-old brother toddled in and sat down to watch the little scene I was enacting. Suddenly, he reached out and snatched my police car that was in hot pursuit of the robbers. I, of course, snatched it back. Naturally, that is the moment my mother walked into the room. My brother spotted

12

her and screamed as if I had punched him. My mother immediately admonished me by saying, "Buddy, don't be selfish. Share with your brother like a good boy!"

The expectations and values we grow up with are insidious, and even the self-diminishing ones can be seductive when they bring approval. Facing our dissatisfactions is complicated because it's scary for us to outgrow the patterns we have learned—to psychologically outgrow our families. Realizing we are doing so may leave us feeling guilty and even ashamed of ourselves. It can also leave us feeling like exiles, without a home or roots or people who care about us and understand us on a basic level.

After loneliness, the second common issue that many of us encounter is the question of what kind of context we can put our parents in during this process. Let me read a couple of paragraphs from *Sacred Selfishness* (p. 58):

> My parents have been dead for many years, yet I think about them every day. The strongest feeling I have when I remember them is one of longing. I yearn to have known them better, to have heard more about their hopes, fears, dreams, struggles, and triumphs. And, I wish they had known me better. I wish they had lived long enough for me to have developed the inner strength it would have taken to risk their anger, to risk upsetting our workable relationship, and to talk openly with them about my childhood and my disappointment, hopes, and dreams. I long to know them deeply and to be known by them.
>
> "Honor your father and mother" was an injunction that served me badly. I have since learned that we must carefully question everything we've been taught to believe as right or wrong, if we are going to live the truth of our own lives. To me, honoring them meant not taking the risk of upsetting them, and this shallow interpretation of the commandment kept me from challenging myself and them into a deeper relationship, one that could truly have honored all

three of us. Nor do I think anyone should "honor" abusive parents because they have already dishonored the sacred trust of being a father or a mother. We must learn to look deeper into how we are living and to listen to how we feel about the principles we're trying to live by.

No matter how difficult things get, we have to remember that establishing our own individual lives is the very foundation for psychological and spiritual development. The symbolic pattern is clear and supports us. Abraham had to leave the country of his father. Buddha had to leave his parents' house. The disciples of Christ had to leave wives, children, and jobs. The same pattern is reflected in fairy tales. Beauty has to leave home, as do Snow White and many others. Our growth depends upon our ability to muster the courage and awareness to separate ourselves from the group mindsets of our families and the conventional wisdom they embody. Then once we have disentangled ourselves, we can decide how we want to relate to them from our own standpoints.

Potential for Growth

I would like to go on and say, however, that developing individual consciousness is also a time of hope and healing. It is a time of discovering the teleological meaning of our symptoms—that's another big word used by Jung to mean the growth our symptoms are trying to point us toward. When we recognize this growth potential, we reconcile our pain with the promise of new life and transformation. And it is a time of joy, of feeling more at home in ourselves as well as in life, a lesson Saint Francis taught the villagers.

This is also a period in an analysand's or a client's process when we as analysts and psychotherapists must be very careful in how we approach our work. If our approach is too structured and/or overly focused on childhood, pathology, or symptoms and dysfunctions—or if we are overly focused on mirroring, interpreting the transference, or even on insight—we can trap the person we are working with in the stage of complex consciousness. And if we do this, we run the risk of limiting our practices to people who are stuck in early wounds. This

14

obstructs our own growth as well. Such focus will move us away from individuation, the teleological value of symptoms, transformation, and our relationship with the Self, no matter how complicated our professional jargon has become in our efforts to explain what we are doing.

The initial progress into individual consciousness reveals the influence of the Self as it pushes us through our conventional attitudes and scripts and complexes and into a unique pattern of growth. During our years of *action*, we have been absorbing the gold of the world that Jung referred to as the "common gold." These have been years of doing, building, becoming, and sometimes healing and accomplishment. But our years of true fruitfulness, of finding the "true gold," in Jung's words, come from reorienting our personalities from *action* to *passion*.

Individual consciousness ushers in a life of passion, and with it the kind of suffering that is creative and transforming. This kind of suffering, which includes the shock of realizing the various aspects of our shadow, differs from healing. Creative suffering becomes most meaningful when we realize, as Jung points out in his autobiography, *Memories, Dreams, Reflections*, that any attempt to live a unique life focused on an individual goal while also adjusting to one's group results in neurosis. For example, many of us were taught by both our actual parents and the world parents that it is a personal failure to even feel, much less acknowledge, the anxiety, vulnerability, and strain built into every life.

In addition, the story of Saint Francis and the wolf always reminds me of how difficult it is to accept our fierceness. I've heard plenty of people who could lecture or talk about shadow work and yet remained caught in the image of the good boy or the good girl they were brought up in. It's one thing to talk about recognizing and owning our shadow; it is something else entirely to get fierce and fight or to own our power when faced with overly demanding parents, partners, children, bosses, or colleagues or when in a divorce or other family or business dispute. We far too easily dread being labeled as troublemakers and allow ourselves to become passive in our depression or paralyzed in our anxiety or panic attacks—or to become inflated in our illusion of goodness when we avoid our power and our fierceness.

15

Illuminated Consciousness

When I sold my business and went back to graduate school, I found myself in a dilemma. The clinical psychology program I wanted to be in was a full-time program taught only in the daytime. At the same time, I had three children to support and didn't want to sacrifice their standard of living to my career change. In other words, I needed to work while I went to school. I was experiencing two conflicting desires and values that seemed to block my direction. In an extraordinarily extroverted moment for me, I found myself sitting in the cafeteria at the university, explaining my predicament to several older students whom I had never seen before. One woman said, "Why don't you try the counseling psychology program?" I had never heard of that program before. As it turned out, it was a well-known, mature department that was much better at training psychotherapists than the clinical program was. It taught day and evening classes and led to many employment opportunities. In fact, what I had done was to hold the tension of opposites—the tension between my desire to become a therapist and my desire to take care of my children—until what Jung calls the transcendent function had a chance to work. I did not give up, get depressed, or rush to any kind of solution. I held the tension until an unusual moment brought a solution that I could not have planned or predicted.

The conflict of duties between conventional or deep personal values and the requirements of individuation are often our clearest challenge for holding the tension of opposites until the transcendent function emerges and opens a new way for us. Holding the tension is a refusal of action that creates a passion of the ego. In such situations, our ego must take a religious attitude of reflection—examining its position, its worldview—and accept the idea that the unconscious can lead us to answers and perspectives that we are not aware of. We must also avoid escaping into passivity or fantasy in our effort to escape suffering or to stay in control. Such passivity is ego control, rather than listening to the Self.

Passion is the way of the Self and leads us into our fourth stage of development, which is called: *illuminated consciousness*. During this stage, our inner work becomes increasingly relational as we seek out a

16

relationship with the Self through our anima and animus. Using the metaphor of the crucifixion, the analyst Edward Edinger in *Ego and Archetype* explains the passion of the ego as an opening to the values of life that transcend the forces that shaped our development. It is also an opening of the heart to a greater love of life and of other people than we have ever imagined and a fruitfulness that inspires hope, confidence, and trust in the hearts of the people around us.

This is the journey into becoming people of substance that I describe in *Sacred Selfishness*. At the end of chapter 11 in that book, I discuss these ideas with Margaret, a woman whose story we have been following. I would like to share the final three paragraphs of this chapter with you:

> As our hour was coming to a close Margaret leaned forward and said, "Looking inward has helped me feel the presence of love in my life. That something has been interested in me all along, guiding my life, supporting it, in some strange way. Trying to become known by me. It's somewhere within myself. It seems funny I had to seek it while at the same time allow it to find me. It brings a sense of peace, or serenity, no matter what hardships I have to face."
>
> When speaking of alchemy, an ancient Chinese writer once said, "They believed that it was a matter of turning lead into gold; was this not madness?" To the practical mind, allowing ourselves to be transformed by the powers of love on its many levels may in fact seem like madness. I've thought so more than once myself. And yet, the ancient alchemists pursued their craft with devotion, separating base materials, refining them, and attempting to bring them back together in a new form.
>
> Margaret learned to live this pattern as a model for her inner work and in her outer relationships. And she discovered, as we all can, a deeper level of being at peace with herself, of experiencing love—of turning ordinary life into gold.

Love, Life, Passion

Jung's work on synchronicity reminds us that the Self is not in the psyche; rather the psyche is in the Self. And the Self is as much in the world as it is involved in our inner processes. As I was considering how to come out of the introverted world of my practice in order to write and then speak to a larger audience, I looked to the thirteenth hexagram in the I Ching as a meditation. In Wilhelm's translation, the title of this hexagram is "Fellowship of Men." R. L. Wing gives this title an updated translation as "Community."

The image of the upper trigram is "The Creative Heaven," and the lower is "The Clinging Flame." Wilhelm notes that it is the nature of fire to flame up to heaven. His comment reminds me that passion means more than suffering. It also means strong desire—a great desire for another, for an idea, for the Divine, for a full life. The flame, according to Wilhelm, gives the idea of fellowship. The "judgment" in this hexagram states, "Fellowship with men in the open. Success." And the text continues, "True fellowship among men must be based on a concern that is universal."

The flame, passion, and love remind us that the imperative of all life is to grow. If we fail to grow, we begin to stagnate and wither, no matter how good the persona we are hiding behind remains. In adult life, this fact leaves us only two choices for the path of our life: that of growth or that of decay. Because we are emotional beings, growth causes anxiety. Transformation, the archetypal pattern of human growth, isn't completely risk free and joyful. Therefore, we are pulled toward individuation, but we are also pulled toward the seeming security of either refusing to grow or of ignoring the possibility of growth. Freud called our pull toward one or the other of these directions the conflict between eros and thanatos.

Erich Fromm described this same conflict as one between a love of life and a love of death. And, incidentally, he felt that our social character is one that loves death. Fromm described the love of death in our culture as the love of objectifying, intellectualizing, quantifying, abstracting, and creating bureaucracies to deal with human problems. To be "normal" in Fromm's perspective is to love death, to be dedicated

18

to a path of spiritual and psychological self-destruction. Jung's position is that we need mythos as the complement to logos, for logos alone will serve the social character by leading to an impersonal life, a life focused on functionality and indifference. Mythos, Jung tells us in *Memories, Dreams, Reflections*, sets life within the context of the heart and of mystery. Individuation is an expression of our love of life. It teaches us that unified and integrated growth serves life. For example, whenever we have recognized and reclaimed one of our shadow projections and integrated its content into our personality, we have served life as well as our own growth.

The path of love is the path of self-knowledge, for this is the only way we can learn to create the conditions for love to take place. And it is the only path that can lead us to understand that love isn't some sentimental ideal. Relationships, if they are to be based on love, require us to strive as hard as we can to overcome indifference. Indifference is a failure to meet the other person and understand his or her reality. In true relationships, our goal isn't to change others in order to satisfy our needs and ideals but to see how knowing others changes us and affects us creatively. Loving life means accepting its wholeness, with its suffering, its failures, and its tragedies. And our challenge is to find consciousness and meaning—in other words, to find the Divine in these experiences.

It also means to accept our responsibility for our part in the transformation of culture. These attitudes lead us to fulfillment, joy, and an experience of unity and illumination. We always face a choice: whether we will allow our souls to congeal into a repetition of what we have done or suffered before or whether we will answer the call from within to become life-givers as long as we are alive.

If we choose to carry the dream of individuation onward, we must bring fully into the open what we think, teach, and stand for. The questions in the human heart articulated by Martin Buber, "Can you teach me to have faith in reality, in the truth of our existence, so that my life will have purpose, meaning, and a way of being fulfilled?" are answered by the journey of individuation. As we mature, it is our job to bring the hope and understanding of this process to the younger generations—in words they can understand, in ways that speak to their struggles and spiritual concerns. And, most importantly, we must teach them that a life being fully lived is creative, loving, and difficult.

Questions to Expand Our Understanding

1. I just shared that "the questions in the human heart articulated by Martin Buber, 'Can you teach me to have faith in reality, in the truth of our existence, so that my life will have purpose, meaning, and a way of being fulfilled?' are answered by the journey of individuation." What are your thoughts and feelings about that?

2. Take time to journal your insights about the journey of individuation.

Chapter 2 : Seminar

SACRED SELFISHNESS:
The Path to Love and Authenticity

Looking in the Mirror

I want to share with you how my interests in spiritual and psychological development originated, how my disillusionment with our cultural idea of "the good life" happened, and the journey these events thrust me into. In my personal reflections, I call this process "looking in the mirror—being face-to-face with myself."

I was born in a part of the country where the religious tradition, whether you belonged to it or not, rooted the culture in the notion of punishment. While I was also taught that God is love, it didn't take me very long to realize that people practiced judgment. By the time I was ten, my little sister had a cancerous Wilms' tumor. By the time I was fourteen, my mother had died a slow death from cancer, and we were left brokenhearted.

In my young mind, the idea that God is love seemed absurd. How could a kind God inflict such pain on us? As a result of my experiences, my childhood concept of God dissolved, leaving me filled with rage and disappointment. Yet at the same time, it was clear that as the disease stripped my mother of everything material, she found increasing comfort in a growing experience of spirituality. Her spiritual development haunted my later efforts to turn my back on the religion that failed me, and it motivated my quest for a spirituality that really mattered. This quest eventually led me to Jung and Zurich.

In my college years, I closed the door on this conflict and shortly thereafter armored myself with ambition. I thought that achieving the good life would heal my past and compensate for my ravaged childhood. By the time I was in my early thirties, my business partner and I owned twelve stores in Atlanta and I was married with three children.

If you had asked me about my inner state, I would have told you that I was a unique person creating his own destiny. But beneath this facade lurked a growing depression and a crumbling marriage. If you had asked me if I loved myself, I would have looked at you kind of funny for even asking such a stupid question and replied, "Of course." The truth is, I didn't really know what the question meant. I didn't understand that if you don't really know someone, what you think of as love can only be an illusion. And this fact applies to ourselves as much as it does to others.

Then, even though I hate to admit it, I wasn't unique either. I was living a pattern that had been formed by the wounds and successes of my childhood and by the training and expectations of my family and society. I thought I was unique. But my depression was telling me that I was an actor in a play that I thought was real life. I was what I refer to in my book *Sacred Selfishness* as a captive of normalcy, and my depression was a call to wake up and begin the journey of discovering an authentic life.

Of course, if we are going to begin such a journey, it's helpful to have a few ideas about what that journey is. My book *Sacred Selfishness* is meant to be a road map for that journey. While climbing out of the hole my life was in during my early thirties, I learned that understanding the most challenging questions—the ones about our purpose, meaning, beauty, God, and love—begins with trying to understand ourselves. Since that day, I have turned to Carl Jung for help. No other spiritual or psychological teacher has provided a model that helped me get to know myself as well as the one that Jung provides. And, as you probably know, his model of the journey is based on our growth in consciousness.

Fundamentally, our society's model of the good life falls into the category that Nietzsche referred to as "sickly selfishness." It teaches us that the normal person wants material prosperity and material security.

This position indoctrinates us into the secret belief that self-interest is primary and that achievement and recognition bring a fulfilling life. Before we know it, we have learned to think of ourselves first, or in some compensatory manner to give ourselves away, in an effort to get other people to show respect, love, and admiration for us.

In contrast to this approach, *Sacred Selfishness* teaches us to follow Jung's path to an authentic life. It teaches us to make the commitment to valuing ourselves enough to become more self-aware and to transform our lives into their fullest expression. The more we grow in this way, the more we end up affecting the world around us for the better, avoiding a "sickness of the soul" and living up to our responsibilities to one another and future generations. The path of *Sacred Selfishness* is a commitment to building the foundation that will support our growing capacity to give and receive love.

Jung taught me—and this is a very important point—that having a religious attitude has nothing to do with a belief system. It means to pay careful attention to our lives, to be attentive to every nuance, to use integrity and intuition as we try to see things clearly, in an effort to see beneath surface appearances. He also taught me to be open to spiritual experiences, those events that through dreams, insight, and reflection help us feel that we are encountering and are even in relationship to something greater than ourselves.

And I must also admit that it was Dr. Jung who helped me become well trained in the habit of prayer, by which I mean the habit of listening carefully. Serious prayer begins with listening for the voice within us. My spiritual practices—and I call them my spiritual practices because they transform my life—were learned from Jung. I give them each a chapter in my book *Sacred Selfishness*. Journaling is a major vehicle for listening to what the voice may be saying through the events in my life and my responses to these events. Befriending my dreams is the way I listen to the inner poetry and drama of my soul. Active imagination is my way of listening to the unknown and often neglected parts of myself.

Dr. Jung also convinced me that self-knowledge is the foundation for discovering the meaning of my inner voice. This voice may, at times, be perceived as a revelation. It may also be a cry from some inner wound that I have repressed and that needs healing or some complex calling for transformation. Once discovered, these aspects of my inner voice always tell me something new and unpredictable—something that when I am aware of it, usually requires obedience, which then means that I must change myself or my life in some way. My practices help me embrace the mystery, and my experience is they can help us all turn our crises into epiphanies, our struggles into inner teachers, and our mistakes into potentials for change that lead to a more complete and satisfying life.

Over forty years of professional training and practice have left me thinking that Jungian psychology and spirituality can be two roads to the same place. Like myself, the people I've worked with believe in love, no matter how bitter and betrayed or cynical they feel. They yearn to feel the presence of the Divine or some spiritual structure that transcends the practicality of our social values and brings a sense of meaning to daily existence.

My early religious training deceived me when I was taught that love was being patient, kind, giving, humble, and generous in degrees without measure and that if my belief was strong enough, I would be able to put this kind of love on like a new shirt. These teachings made me feel like a failure from a very early age. But now I've learned that love isn't this simple and to think it is trivializes it, makes it shallow and frivolous, because we know life isn't this simple, and so love can't be either. We need to remember that the mystics in every great religion believe love is the measure of all things, and they pursue a long road before being able to experience the Divine as love.

It might also be helpful to remember the journey that made up the life of Saint Paul, who so beautifully wrote in 1 Corinthians, chapter 13, that love is the measure of all things, greater than faith and deeds. A storm-driven man with blood on his hands, Saint Paul had been brought to his knees and had a fear of sex and women. He was a man who pursued his life wholeheartedly, made many mistakes, had to confront his own dark side, suffered much, and thereby gained the wisdom that led him to his conclusions about love.

Love becomes real once we see through the fog of our illusions, look upon ourselves face-to-face, and realize that the spiritual quest is to become fully human. Learning to know ourselves teaches us how love and becomes the measure of all things. Now, I have presented some fairly intense ideas to you. I want you to take a moment, maybe take a deep breath.

Questions to Expand Our Understanding

1. Did anything I said make you feel uncomfortable?
2. Did anything make you feel engaged or energized?
3. Were you surprised at any point?

A Way of Being Fulfilled

My purpose in all of my lectures and writings has been to present Jung's work in a clear manner. I've done this in an effort to clarify these paths for all of us who are living in a busy world and who would like to find a spiritual or psychological orientation that supports a fulfilling life. Martin Buber articulated the questions we desire to have answered: "Can you teach me to have faith in reality, in the truth of our existence, so that my life will have purpose, meaning, and a way of being fulfilled?"

These questions come from a mysterious source within us. We can cope with life, manage our affairs, and be successful in a conventional sense. And yet this mysterious longing persists. The uncertainty of life is also a mystery. Longing and uncertainty keep us on the edge—keep us awake, alive, aware—and urge us to pay greater attention to who we are and how we are living. The path of individuation that Jung lays out for us depends on attention and awareness. And as many of you know, he uses the development of consciousness as a guide for understanding how our personality develops.

In *Sacred Selfishness*, I use a fairly simple illustration to outline the Jungian point of view in terms of the stages of individuation.

The Four Stages of Consciousness

The first stage is simple consciousness. It is the naïve, developing consciousness of childhood. This period of time begins with birth and encompasses the years of our early lives, when our ability to learn and act responsibly is a potential slowly being fulfilled. Our parents, families, schools, churches, places in society, and the media introduce us to life in the world.

The second stage is complex consciousness. Complex consciousness is the consciousness required to fulfill the societal tasks of adulthood. This stage develops as we grow through adolescence into adulthood. During this stage we become aware of the attempt to undertake the social and personal tasks that generally define adulthood.

The third stage is individual consciousness. Individual consciousness is the awareness of ourselves as separate from the forces that molded us. It is as if a door were opening, inviting us into the experience of personal authenticity and of feeling truly at home within ourselves.

The fourth stage is illuminated consciousness. This final stage includes the realization of our unique personalities and their relationship to our deeper Selves and all life.

"If we don't know ourselves, the best we can do is love a fantasy of who we are, a contrivance, an image or illusion. To know ourselves, we must break free enough of the influences in our pasts to recognize the parts of ourselves we've denied and to begin to accept our authentic characteristics—those we like and those we don't like."

— from *Sacred Selfishness: A Guide to Living a Life of Substance*

So, we begin with the development of simple consciousness, and as we grow through adolescence and into adulthood, we grow into complex consciousness, which is considered normal adulthood. As we progress into normal adulthood, three forces influence our development: (1) our biological inheritance; (2) the inspirations, wounds, and traumas of our childhood; and (3) the social character of our times.

I want to focus on the third force, the social character of our times, because it not only determines what we think of as normal in our culture but also influences much of what we experience as childhood wounds and inspirations. Let me remind you that the psychoanalyst Erich Fromm coined the term *social character* and defined it by saying that every society develops the image of a model person needed to keep its values and institutions working. In turn, society's institutions—such as the family, schools, churches, the media, and advertising—attempt to mold our development into a personality that fits the model of our society's social character. Therefore, the social character of our culture provides the fundamental traits we identify with and becomes the foundation of our identity as well as the definition of what is normal.

Questions to Expand Our Understanding

Now I would like to ask you to make these ideas more personal. Let's consider this quote: "Knowing yourself, really knowing yourself, requires recognizing how you are a 'captive of normalcy' and may be trapped in your identity. You must examine the past."

1. Take five minutes and make a list of beliefs. Then see what reflections you come up with.

2. What kinds of feelings came up in you?

3. Were you surprised?

There are two reasons that I have emphasized social character so much. First, it guides the development of our personality—the personality that we need to be strong in order to function in the world and that serves as the foundation for our individuation. And, second, we have to become aware that however strong and successful our personality is initially, it isn't necessarily authentic on the personal level.

Facing the Dark and Finding Life

Let's read a fairy tale and see what it can tell us about authenticity. As you may know, we begin to find our authenticity by looking into our shadows. To help do this, I am going to share a shortened version of the fairy tale titled "The Shadow." This is one of my favorite tales. In fact, I used this fairy tale to open the chapter in *Sacred Selfishness* called "Facing the Dark and Finding Life." This story may even show us how we have severed and banished from our personalities the ability to truly experience life. Our social character and its shallow ideals exert enough force to put our instinctual wolf in a cage.

THE SEARCH FOR SELF AND THE SEARCH FOR GOD

You may be aware that we build our shadows as we build our identities. In *Sacred Selfishness* (p. 244), I say, "They're like two sides of the same coin. Every time we identify with a value such as 'It's good to be active and efficient,' we reject its opposite—it's as if we've said, 'It's bad to be lazy and lackadaisical.' Eventually our identities are based on collections of such identifications and they define who we believe we are."

Now let's see what happens to a man who wants to devote his life to the good, the true, and the beautiful in this fairy tale from Hans Christian Andersen.

The Shadow

A learned man once traveled to a very hot climate where the heat of the sun has great power. He found that he must remain in the house during the day, because the sun became quite unbearable. It seemed to the learned man as if he were sitting in an oven, and he became quite exhausted and weak, and grew so thin that his shadow shriveled up. He saw nothing of it till after sunset. It was really a pleasure, as soon as the lights were brought into the room, to see the shadow stretch itself to the ceiling to recover its strength. The learned man would sometimes go out onto the balcony to stretch himself also and feel revived. People at this hour began to make their appearance in all the balconies in the street, for in warm climates every house has a balcony, in which they can breathe the fresh evening air. In the street beneath, they brought out tables and chairs, lighted candles by hundreds, talked and sang, and were merry. One house only, which was just opposite to his, formed a contrast to all this, for it was quite still. Yet somebody dwelt there, for flowers stood in the balcony, blooming beautifully in the hot sun and this could not have been, unless they had been watered carefully. The doors leading to the balcony were half opened in the evening and music could be heard from the interior of the house. The music was so lovely that it produced the most enchanting thoughts, and acted on the senses with magic power.

Once the foreigner woke in the night, and there appeared a wonderful brightness over the balcony of the opposite house. Among the flowers stood a beautiful slender maiden. It was as if light streamed from her and dazzled his eyes. He crept softly behind the curtain, but she was gone.

28

One evening the foreigner sat on the balcony with a light burning just behind him. It was quite natural, therefore, that his shadow should fall on the wall of the opposite house, so that as he sat amongst the flowers on his balcony, when he moved, his shadow moved also.

"I think my shadow ought to be clever enough to step in, and then come back and tell me what he has seen," said the learned man. And if anyone had observed, they might have seen the shadow go straight into the half-opened door of the opposite balcony.

The next morning the shadow had not yet returned, and in the evening the learned man went out again on his balcony, taking care to place the light behind him for he knew that a shadow always wants his master for a screen. He made himself little, and he made himself tall, but no shadow came. That was very vexing, but in warm countries everything grows very quickly and after a week had passed, he saw, to his great joy, that a new shadow was growing from his feet...as if a root had remained. After three weeks, he had quite a respectable shadow which, during his return journey to northern lands, continued to grow and became so large that he might very well have spared half of it. When this learned man arrived back home, he wrote books about the true, the good and the beautiful, which are to be found in this world, and so days and years passed.

One evening, as he sat in his study, a very gentle tap was heard at the door. He opened the door, and there stood before him a man so remarkably thin that he felt seriously troubled at his appearance. He was, however, very well-dressed, and looked like a gentleman. "To whom have I the honor of speaking?" said he.

"Ah, I hoped you would recognize me," said the elegant stranger, "I have gained so much, that I have a body of flesh and clothes to wear. Do you not recognize your old shadow? All has been prosperous with me since I was with you last, and were I inclined to purchase my freedom from service, I could easily do so."

"I cannot recover from my astonishment," said the learned man. "What does all this mean?"

"Something rather unusual," said the shadow, "But you are yourself an uncommon man, and you know very well that I have followed in your footsteps ever since your childhood. As soon as you found that I had traveled

29

enough to be trusted alone, I went my own way, and I am now in the most brilliant circumstances. But I felt a kind of longing to see you once more before you die, for there is always a clinging to the land of one's birth."

"Well this is most remarkable," said the learned man. "I never supposed that a man's old shadow could become a human being."

"Just tell me what I owe you," said the shadow, "for I do not like to be in debt to any man."

"What question of debt can there be between us?" said the learned man. "You are as free as any one. I rejoice exceedingly to hear of your good fortune. Sit down, old friend, and tell me how it happened, and what you saw in the house opposite to me while we were in those hot climates."

"First you must promise me never to tell that I have been your shadow. I am thinking of being married."

"Here is my hand—I promise, and a word is sufficient between man and man." It was really most remarkable how very much he had become a man in appearance.

"Now I will relate to you what you wish to know," said the shadow, placing his foot as firmly as possible on the arm of the new shadow of the learned man, which lay at his feet like a poodle dog. The new shadow remained quiet and at rest, for it wanted to know how a shadow could be sent away by its master and become a man itself.

"In the house opposite to you, lived the most glorious creature in the world. It was poetry," said the shadow. "I remained there three weeks, and it was more like three thousand years, for I read all that has ever been written. In truth, I saw and learned everything."

"Poetry!" exclaimed the learned man. "Yes, I saw her once for a very short moment, while sleep weighed down my eyelids. She flashed upon me from the balcony like the radiant aurora borealis, surrounded with flowers like flames of fire. Tell me...you were on the balcony that evening...you went through the door, and what didst thou see?"

"I saw everything, as you shall hear. But I wish you would say 'you' to me instead of 'thou.'"

"I beg your pardon," said the learned man. "It is an old habit, which is difficult to break. But now tell me everything that you saw. What was the appearance of the inner room? Was it there like a cool grove, or like a

holy temple? Were the chambers like a starry sky seen from the top of a high mountain?"

"It was all that you describe," said the shadow, "but I did not go quite in, for the blaze of light would have killed me, had I approached too near the maiden myself, but I could see and hear all that was going on in the court of poetry."

"But what did you see? Did the gods of ancient times pass through the rooms? Did old heroes fight their battles over again? Were there lovely children at play, who related their dreams?"

"You may be sure that I saw everything that was to be seen. If you had gone there, you would not have remained a human being, whereas I became one...and at the same moment, I became aware of my inner being, my inborn affinity to the nature of poetry. It is true I did not think much about it while I was with you, for I did not then understand my inner existence. But in the anteroom it was revealed to me. I became a man. I came out in full maturity. But you had left the warm countries by then. And as a man, I felt ashamed to go about without boots or clothes and that exterior finish by which a man is known. So I went my own way. I hid myself under the cloak of a cake woman, but she little thought whom she concealed. It was not till evening that I ventured out. I ran here and there, looked through the highest windows into the rooms, and over the roofs. I saw what nobody else could see. Miserable things going on between husbands and wives, parents and children, and the evil conduct of their neighbors. Had I written a newspaper, how eagerly it would have been read! Instead I wrote directly to the persons themselves, and great alarm arose in all the towns I visited. They had so much fear of me, and yet how dearly they loved me. The professor made me a professor. The tailor gave me new clothes. The overseer of the mint struck coins for me. The women declared that I was handsome, and so I became the man you now see. And now I must say adieu." And the shadow departed.

Years passed, and the shadow came again. "How are you going on now?" he asked.

"I am writing about the true, the beautiful, and the good...but no one cares," said the learned man. "I am quite in despair, for I take it to heart very much."

"You do not understand the world," said the shadow. "You will make yourself ill about it. You ought to travel. I am going on a journey in the summer. Will you travel with me as my shadow? It would give me great pleasure, and I will pay all the expenses."

The learned man was hesitant and the shadow went away.

Afterwards, everything went wrong with the learned man. Sorrow and trouble pursued him, and what he said about the good, the beautiful, and the true was of as much value to most people as a nutmeg would be to a cow. At length he fell ill. "You really look like a shadow," people said to him, and a cold shudder would pass over him.

On this next visit, the shadow insisted that he take a trip. "There is no other chance for you. I will take you with me, for the sake of old acquaintance. I will pay the expenses of your journey, and you shall write a description of it to amuse us by the way."

At last they started together. The shadow was master now, and the master became the shadow. They drove together and walked side by side, or one in front and the other behind, according to the position of the sun. The shadow always knew when to take the place of honor, but the learned man took no notice of it for he had a good heart and was exceedingly mild and friendly.

One day the master said to the shadow, "We have grown up together from childhood, and now that we have become traveling companions, shall we not drink to our good fellowship, and say 'thee' and 'thou' to each other?"

"What you say is very straightforward and kindly," said the shadow who was now really master. "I will be equally kind and straightforward. I cannot allow you to say 'thou' to me. I feel crushed by it, as I used to feel in my former position with you. I will gladly say it to you, and therefore your wish will be half fulfilled." Then the shadow addressed his former master as "thou."

"It is going rather too far," said the latter, "that I am to say 'you' when I speak to him, and he is to say 'thou' to me." However, he was obliged to submit.

They arrived at the baths where there were many strangers, and among them a beautiful princess, whose real disease consisted in being too sharp-sighted, which made every one very uneasy. One day she entered into con-

versation with the strange gentleman. Being a princess, she was not obliged to stand upon much ceremony, so she said to him without hesitation, "Your illness consists in you not being able to cast a shadow."

"Your royal highness must be on the high road to recovery from your illness," said he. "I know your complaint arose from being too sharp-sighted, and in this case it has entirely failed. I happen to have the most unusual shadow. Have you not seen a person who is always at my side? I had dressed out my shadow like a man, and you may observe that I have even given him a shadow of his own. It is rather expensive, but I like to have things about me that are peculiar."

"This foreign prince—for he must be a prince—pleases me above all things," thought the princess.

In the evening, the princess and the shadow danced together in the large assembly rooms. She was light, but he was lighter still. She had never seen such a dancer before. She told him from what country she had come, and found he knew it and had been there, but not while she was at home. He had looked into the windows of her father's palace, both the upper and lower windows. He had seen many things, and could therefore make allusions which quite astonished her. She thought he must be the cleverest man in all the world, and felt the greatest respect for his knowledge. When she danced with him again, she fell in love with him. "He is a clever man," she thought to herself, "which is a good thing, and he dances admirably, which is also good. But has he well-grounded knowledge?" Then she asked him a most difficult question that she herself could not have answered.

"I learned something about it in my childhood," he replied, "and I believe that even my shadow, standing over there by the door, could answer it. He has followed me for so many years, and has heard so much from me, that I think it is very likely. But he is very proud of being considered a man; so that he may answer correctly, he must be treated as a man."

"I shall be pleased to do so," said the princess. So she walked up to the learned man, who stood in the doorway, and spoke to him, and the learned man conversed with her pleasantly and sensibly.

"What a wonderful man he must be to have such a clever shadow!" thought she. "If I were to choose him, it would be a blessing to my country *and my subjects." So the princess and the shadow were soon engaged.*

"Listen my friend," said the shadow to the learned man, "Now that I am as fortunate and powerful as any man can be, I will do something unusually good for you. You shall live in my palace, drive with me in the royal carriage, and have a hundred thousand dollars a year, but you must allow everyone to call you a shadow, and never venture to say that you have been a man. And once a year, when I sit on my balcony in the sunshine, you must lie at my feet as becomes a shadow to do for I am going to marry the princess, and our wedding will take place this evening."

"Now, really, this is too ridiculous," said the learned man. "I will disclose everything, and say that I am the man, and that you are only a shadow dressed up in men's clothes."

"No one will believe you," said the shadow. "Be reasonable, now, or I will call the guards."

"I will go straight to the princess," said the learned man.

"But I shall be there first," replied the shadow, "and you will be sent to prison." And so it turned out, for the guards readily obeyed him, as they knew he was going to marry the king's daughter.

"You tremble," said the princess, when the shadow appeared before her.

"I have gone through a most terrible affair," said the shadow. "My shadow has gone mad. He fancies that he has become a real man, and that I am his shadow."

"How very terrible," cried the princess. "Is he locked up?"

"Oh yes, certainly, for I fear he will never recover."

"Poor shadow!" said the princess, "It is very unfortunate for him. It would really be a good deed to free him from his frail existence and, indeed, put him out of the way quietly."

"It is certainly rather hard upon him, for he was a faithful servant," said the shadow, and he pretended to sigh.

"Yours is a noble character," said the princess, and bowed herself before him.

In the evening the whole town was illuminated, and it was indeed a grand wedding. But the learned man heard nothing of all these festivities, for he had already been executed.

Questions for Reflection

1. As you are thinking about the story, write down the image or images that affected you the most.

2. Now I would like for you to reflect for a few more minutes and write down the feelings, ideas, and questions the story brought up in you.

3. How did this story remind you of parts of your own unlived life?

I say in *Sacred Selfishness* that there are two themes that seem to come into perspective in the story. The first theme is of separation—the scholar, though fascinated with his shadow, is quite comfortable staying separate or apart from his shadow. Often, it seems more comfortable to keep a safe distance from life, rather than to risk the tumultuous effects it can have on us when we become passionately involved in it. The second theme is life's attraction toward the shadow, which becomes enriched by it, and this theme continues.

Questions to Expand Our Understanding

1. Think about the first theme. How do you see this kind of separation happening to people every day?

2. What are some of your experiences of the situation in the second theme—how life seems attracted to the shadow, which becomes enriched by it?

3. To what use can you put the information we've been talking about?

4. Do these ideas give you any insight into our collective consciousness?

5. What are you learning about our shadows, about how we split ourselves, and about what this might do to our capacity to live with vitality?

The Descent

In talking about the fairy tale "The Shadow," we saw how the learned man's insistence on holding on to the external social values of the true, the good, and the beautiful caused him to become one-sided in his approach to life. This story reminds us that the values of our social character are always incomplete and will cause us to live inauthentic lives.

In my spring 2009 e-newsletter, I describe a dream in which an angry, anguished woman is rushing at me with a butcher knife. She wants to make me feel her pain. She belongs to the intangible world of my unconscious—a world that our social character sees as almost valueless. For those of us who want to heal ourselves and pursue spiritual growth and individuation, we have to deal with the fear and bias of our social character, which negates the inner world and refuses to acknowledge any value in it.

What this means to us personally is the fear that other people will think we are weird or strange when we devote time or energy to our inner work, or our own internal critic will say that we are being self-indulgent, wasting our time, and not being productive. Yet in all of our great mystical and mythological traditions, it is the painful process of stripping ourselves of the values of our social character that heals our deepest wounds and becomes the foundation for authenticity, growth, wisdom, and love. One of our earliest myths, the one of the descent into the underworld of the goddess Inanna, can help us understand our own journey into wholeness.

So, let's spend a few minutes reflecting on this myth, and I will begin by sharing my version of it with you.

Inanna's Descent

In the ancient Sumerian myth, Inanna has evolved through three stories or chapters to the peak of her powers as the queen of heaven and earth. In her first myth or story, she has gone through the ordeals necessary to acquire her throne and bed, symbolizing her sovereignty and queenship. In her second myth, she uses guile to acquire orderliness and the attributes of civilization from Enki, the god of wisdom and waters. Ultimately, she shares these attributes with humanity and hastens the development of civilization. In the third myth, Inanna brings together the masculine and the feminine when she takes the shepherd, Dumuzi, as her consort and makes him king. She then becomes a mother as well, when she gives birth to two sons.

In these first three myths, Inanna has gone through what we might refer to as ego development, or the maturing to the stage of complex consciousness that we have discussed. These first three myths represent her journey up to

36

the point of her fourth myth, the "Descent into the Underworld." This is the most well-known myth about Inanna; it recounts the journey necessary to take her into what I've called individual consciousness, or personal authenticity.

Inanna's descent into the underworld begins when she opens her ear to the Great Below. We know that the Sumerian word for ear was the same as that for wisdom, but we don't know what kind of call compelled Inanna to undertake this next quest on her perilous journey. We do know that she decided she needed to descend into the underworld. Her court and people pleaded with her not to make this journey because the underworld was ruled by Inanna's vicious sister, Ereshkigal, queen of the Great Below. This was a very dangerous place and many of those who journeyed there never returned.

As the story slowly begins, Inanna abandons her temples in the seven cities of her kingdom, along with all of the glories of heaven and earth. She gathers together the seven attributes of civilization and transforms them into symbols of her surface power and prestige. These become seven items: her royal crown, her lapis necklace and earrings, her gold breastplate, her golden wrist band, the golden wrist band on her other hand, the lapis rod of office, and her royal robe. She feels that these symbols of her queenship will protect her. But being aware of the danger in her journey, she instructs her female assistant Ninshubur to appeal to the father gods for help if she doesn't return in three days.

When Inanna arrives at the outer gates of the Underworld, she announces herself as "Inanna, the Queen of Heaven, on my way to the East." Neti, the chief gatekeeper of the underworld, is skeptical and begins to question her further. In response to his questions, Inanna replies that she wishes to descend because of her older sister, Ereshkigal, and to witness the funeral rites of Ereshkigal's husband, Gugalanna. Neti is still uncertain and he tells Inanna to wait while he consults with Ereshkigal.

When Neti tells Queen Ereshkigal that Inanna is at the main gate to the Great Below (or the Underworld) clothed in the seven attributes of her glory as queen of heaven, Ereshkigal is furious. After reflecting on this news for some time, she instructs Neti to bolt the seven gates of the Underworld and then to allow Inanna to enter slowly through one gate at a time. As she passes through each gate, Neti is to remove her royal symbols, one at a time. Ereshkigal tells Neti to let the queen of heaven enter the Underworld "bowed low."

Neti follows his queen's instructions by bolting the seven gates to the Underworld and then allowing Inanna to enter slowly through one gate at a time. As Inanna stops at each gate, Neti removes one of her symbols of power. He begins with her crown and then continues to remove her lapis necklace and earrings, gold breastplate, golden wrist bands, the lapis rod of her sovereignty, and then, at the last gate, her royal robe. At each gate Inanna asks, "What is this?"

Neti replies, "Quiet, Inanna, the ways of the Underworld are perfect. They may not be questioned."

Finally, naked and bowed low, Inanna enters the throne room of her dark sister. Ereshkigal rises from her throne as Inanna approaches her. The Annuna, the judges in the Underworld, also arise. They surround Inanna and pass judgment against her. Then Ereshkigal fastens "the eyes of death" on Inanna, screaming her wrath and her accusations of guilt at her, finally striking her as well. With this blow, Inanna turns into a corpse, a piece of rotting meat, and she is hung from a hook on the wall. While Inanna is in this state in the Underworld, the upper earth is barren and nothing grows or reproduces.

After three days and nights, when Inanna has not returned, her assistant Ninshubur becomes alarmed. She begins to cry out and beat the drum for Inanna. In desperation, she goes to Inanna's paternal grandfather, Enlil, and then to Inanna's father, Nanna, pleading for help. She begs them not to let their daughter die in the Underworld. But both of them refuse to help Inanna because they don't appreciate or even understand the journey she has undertaken.

Then Ninshubur goes to Enki, the god of wisdom and waters that Inanna previously tricked to get the attributes of civilization. Enki is Inanna's mother's father. In spite of their history, Enki is troubled and grieved for Inanna.

At the same time, Ereshkigal is moaning with the cries of a woman about to give birth, for she is pregnant. She is in great pain and is complaining about pain that is both inside and outside.

Aware of her pain, Enki wisely takes the dirt from under his fingernails and creates two small creatures the size of flies. They are the Kurgarra and the Galatur, two professional mourners capable of mirroring lonely Eresh-kigal's emotions. These two small creatures also carry the water and food of life.

Following Enki's instructions, the Kurgarra and the Galatur enter into the underworld as flies. They approach Ereshkigal, who is moaning with great pain as she is about to give birth. She complains about her inside and her outside, her back, her heart, and her liver. Every time she expresses her pain, the Kurgarra and the Galatur absorb and echo it. By their concern, they are able to calm the pain of the anguished queen and she becomes will-ing to offer them fertility and growth in return for their compassion. First, she offered her blessings, the river in its fullness and then the fields ready for the harvest. But each time, the Kurgarra and the Galatur turn her down. Finally, Ereshkigal asks them what they want. They reply that they want the corpse on the hook. Ereshkigal gives them the corpse. Then they sprinkle the food and water of life on Inanna and she is restored to life.

When Inanna is about to ascend from the Underworld, the Annuna seize her and tell her she must provide someone to take her place. They send the galla, the demons of the underworld, back with Inanna. They are to stay by her side until she chooses someone they can take back to the under-world.

As Inanna comes out of the gates of the Underworld, Ninshubur, dressed in soiled sackcloth, throws herself at Inanna's feet. The galla are willing to take Ninshubur, but Inanna refuses because she knows of Nin-shubur's support and the part she played in her rescue. Inanna also refuses to send her sons, who had mourned for her death. But when Inanna arrives in her palace, she finds her husband, Dumuzi, sitting on his throne enjoy-ing the power his wife had given him and not very concerned about her welfare. So, Inanna instructs the galla to take him back to the Underworld.

Dumuzi tries to escape by having the god Utu turn him into a snake and then a gazelle. But each time the galla find him. Dumuzi seeks help from his wise sister, Geshtinanna, after having a terrible dream. She predicts a tragic fate for both of them. Even though she tries to protect Dumuzi, the galla find him and take him to the Underworld.

In deep mourning, Geshtinanna cries out that she will share her brother's fate. Inanna, moved by such grief and her former love for Dumuzi, intervenes and arranges with Ereshkigal that Dumuzi and Geshtinanna will each go to the Underworld for half the year and that each will spend the other half of the year in the world above. Then Inanna places both of them in the "hands of the eternal," which makes them immortal. The myth ends with hymns of praise sung to holy Ereshkigal and her great renown.

Questions for Reflection

As you are still reflecting upon the story, let me ask you a few questions about it.

1. Was anything in the story puzzling to you?
2. Did any part of it cause you to feel uncomfortable?
3. Where did you feel energized or engaged?
4. What associations did you make with the story?
5. How did you feel at the end of the story?

Of course, one thing we always need to ask ourselves is, how is this story relevant to my life right now? Regarding this particular story, let's examine what it really means to go into the Underworld. It means to put our persona aside and to put aside the rules of our culture that try to make us appear good, strong, happy, and in control. It is using our journals to ask ourselves questions such as these:

1. What is my greatest fear?
2. What are the characteristics of that person I hate—or the terrorist, the horrible animal, and so on—that showed up in my dream? And how are these characteristics part of me?
3. What am I most afraid to tell my mother, my father, or my partner?
4. What are all the reasons why I'm scared to write down the secrets in my life and family—both my family of origin and my current family?
5. Who is the person in my life who scares me the most?
6. Whose criticism do I fear the most?

These questions are only a few examples. But if you consider them or some others you may have thought of, two things may occur to you. First, with everything we write, we feel lighter, and when we have expressed something authentic that has been hidden, we become more authentic. Second, we begin to discover the potential for compassion for ourselves. The Kurgarra and the Galatur from the myth, the professional mourners, are the carriers of the archetypal source of inner compassion.

A descent is always an initiation. Almost without our realizing it, our old view of ourselves will change, and our callous attitude toward our own suffering will change.

Questions for Reflection

In order to help us explore our thoughts about the Underworld, I would like for you to read this paragraph and then write some of your reflections and feelings about it:

"We must be able to be with our own pain, to accept it and move through it slowly so healing can occur. There is no place in the Underworld for coldness toward our own suffering, no room for expectations of invulnerability, or denial of our wounds. In the Underworld suffering is respected, pain is *allowed and life is real.*"

Growth and Self-Love

Now we are going to change our pace, leave the Underworld, and focus more on growth and self-love. Cultivating growth and self-love is an art, and it is part of the journey. Both involve knowing ourselves better and learning to accept and deal with what we discover within ourselves.

Quotations for Reflection

In order to help us explore growth and self-love further, I would like for you to read the quotations below. Then write your reflections about each one.

Self-forgiveness rests on being able to understand who we were at the time, and what needs, hurts, fears, and deprivations were driving us. Only then may we meet ourselves with compassion and kindness. Growth in self-knowledge brings healing, and atonement in its deepest sense means to become "at one" with who we are, to reconcile through love with our essential selves. Our capacity to do this leads us back to the ability to say "I am human" in its full spiritual sense.

(*Sacred Selfishness*, p. 277)

Self-love is the firm foundation that determines how strongly we can give love and receive love. Without it our structures of relationship will crumble under the pressure of the smallest storm. Self-love is neither selfish nor narcissistic.

(*Sacred Selfishness*, p. 273)

At the beginning of my lecture in Chapter 1, I asked you to keep the following three questions in mind. As you may recall, these questions come up whenever we have to make a choice.

1. Will this decision contribute to my self-love?
2. Will this decision contribute to my individuation process—my process of authentic growth and development?
3. What do you think about the ethics of the first two questions? Are these questions a sign of being good or bad, selfish or unselfish, profound, or what?

I would now like to add two more questions to this list:

4. Do not ask, do I love myself? Instead, ask the question, can I give myself the love that I need?
5. Do not ask, what do I do to be good? Instead, ask the question, how do I live to bring meaning to my life?

Questions for Reflection

Take time to reflect about all five of the questions above and write your thoughts and feelings about each of them. Then come back to these questions later and continue to journal your reflections.

STEPS TO AN AUTHENTIC LIFE

Do You Really Feel Your Emotions?

In order to be a person of substance and be true to your inner being, you have to authentically feel your feelings. But through the course of the years, many of us learn to barricade ourselves and to wall off our feelings, and we don't even know it.

One of the first steps to living an authentic life is to know if you are really experiencing your emotions. If you are doing any of the following, you may be walling off your feelings:

HAVING AN ABSENCE OF FEELINGS A lack of feelings, usually a coolness or remoteness, based on the mistaken belief that it is generally better to be non-emotional and objective

BEING OVERLY SENTIMENTAL An excess of ungrounded or undifferentiated feelings that come up unexpectedly or in outbursts

HAVING MOOD STATES Inexplicably going from high to low or dropping into touchiness, sulkiness, self-criticism, criticism, or vulnerability

Learn to Relate to Yourself

If you find you are blocking your emotions, there are things you can do to feel more deeply.

Four Simple Steps to Relate Better to Yourself:

PAY ATTENTION Pay attention to what you experience. The more you pay attention, the more you will realize that everything—thoughts, feelings, dreams, outer life, and physical symptoms—in your life is important and warrants your time and attention.

LISTEN OPENLY Listen openly to yourself and others. That means cultivating the ability to set aside your own point of view in order to fully understand that of others—including your inner Self.

QUESTION Question what's really going on around you, both in your inner and outer worlds. Remember to be gentle.

REFLECT Reflect on your life and on what you have learned by the first three steps. Journaling is a good way to reflect.

PART TWO

FIRE IN THE SOUL: A Jungian Guide to Discovering the Promise in Our Holy Longing

"People speak of belief when they have lost knowledge. Belief and disbelief in God are mere surrogates. The naïve primitive doesn't believe, he knows, because the inner experience rightly means as much to him as the outer."

— C. G. JUNG, C. W. VOL. 2, 13 FEB. 1952

"What we need is a new point of departure and this cannot be found without the assignment of new meaning. The message is alive only if it creates new meaning. I don't believe at all that it has run dry, rather that theology has. Just how do you make it clear to your listeners that 'the death and resurrection of Christ are their death and resurrection'?"

— C. G. JUNG, C. W. VOL. 2, 23 SEPT. 1952

"Christ forces man into the impossible conflict. He took himself with exemplary seriousness and lived his life to the bitter end, regardless of human convention and in opposition to his own lawful tradition, as the worst heretic in the eyes of the Jews and a madman in the eyes of his family."

— C. G. JUNG, C. W. VOL. 2, 3 JULY 1952

"If you try to be literal about the doctrine, you are putting yourself aside until there is nobody left that would represent it but corpses. If on the other hand, you truly assimilate the doctrine, you will alter it creatively by your individual understanding and thus give it life."

— C. G. JUNG, C. W. VOL. 2, 10 APRIL 1954

"If one is unwilling to take on the challenge of engagement with the larger Self, then we experience the truth of Jung's observation that service to our neurosis becomes our unconscious religion."

— JAMES HOLLIS, QUADRANT, XXXVI: 2, 13

Chapter 3 : Lecture

FIRE IN THE SOUL:
A Jungian Guide to Discovering the Promise in Our Holy Longing

I am pleased to have this opportunity to share some of my thoughts about the promises in our Holy Longing and how important these longings are to both our spiritual journeys and our individuation processes. I am going to divide this lecture into two parts. In the first part I will talk about longing, awaking, desire, and the failure of our religious institutions, and I will describe why religion and spirituality need each other. Then I will proceed with the next section of the lecture, which will amplify the mystic journey and individuation and illustrate what these processes can mean to our lives and how they can help us be spiritually engaged in life through a process that awakens our deepest potentials for love, hope, and fulfillment.

This topic represents a deep, personal journey of my own. And while I will be talking about Jungian psychology, the mystical process, religion, and spirituality, I will also be talking about myself because that's where my search began.

Our Longings and Our Fears

Most of us don't feel compelled to look into bigger questions until our life isn't working, or until we are haunted by the feeling that something is missing, or until the bottom falls out and we are face to face with the big questions: Who am I? Why am I here? What can all this mean?

Then we begin longing for answers while at the same time, in most cases, we are trying to defend ourselves against our longings and our fears—because these very longings will often touch some of our most basic fears and wounds.

Regarding the area of religion, Jung was very aware of the longing in the human hearts of modern people. The Jewish theologian Martin Buber expresses this longing by asking the following question of religion: "Can you teach me to have faith in reality, in the truth of our existence, so that my life will have purpose, meaning, and a way of being fulfilled?" This question articulates a very sophisticated kind of longing.

The Jungian analyst Dr. James Hillman, in his discussion of abandonment, takes our longing to its most basic level. For some of us, it is "Help! Please help me." Others say, "Take me, just as I am, no judgments or questions asked," or "Take me without my having to do something, or be someone." Another one of us may cry out, "Hold me," or "Don't go away. Never leave me alone." Dr. Hillman suggests that we may hear the content of these pleas as saying simply, "Love me." Or we can hear, "Teach me, guide me, show me what to do, or tell me how," or "Carry me, keep me," or the cry from the hopelessness in our soul which says, "Leave me alone. Just let me be."

These are the longings of the archetypal child within us. They are never satisfied. And while we may experience them in our woundedness and our addictions, even when these are healed, the longings of the archetypal child within us will continue fueling the more sophisticated longings expressed by Martin Buber. At this point we can begin to sense that our longings are also an expression of our eternal vulnerability. But they are also an expression of the future potentials of this archetype that lives within us and wants our life to be creative as long as we are alive. And if we do not seek to become whole and serve something larger than ourselves—to be creating and re-creating our lives—this archetype will push us and even punish us with its longings.

It is helpful for us to consider that though they may drive us, our longings are a passive state, maybe even an infantile state at times. In order to help this state become active, we must accept it, own it, and become involved with it, which means living into the feelings it brings. When our longing is welcomed, when it is invited to touch and move our souls, it becomes transformed into desire. And that is when our desire becomes holy.

In my book *The Fire and the Rose*, I say that desire, whether it's for another person or the Divine, is a hunger to participate in life on a more intense level than we can achieve on our own. Ultimately, I believe desire must be for participation—for engagement—and not for possession; otherwise we will end up destroying the experience we are seeking. In its fullest sense, desire is a longing to involve ourselves in the spirit and the body of the world. Through the body—which means through our senses, feelings, and thoughts—desire pours itself into our experiences. Through self-awareness and reflection, we are able to open our heart's deepest secrets in order to allow our desire to become creative and to make our lives richer and increasingly meaningful.

If we have the courage to remain open, our desire will give birth to passion. If we are timid and overly careful, our passion will wear the disguise of fear, disparagement, or even envy and resentment. Passion is both a longing for and a feeling of being compelled toward someone or something outside of ourselves. Passion arouses us to action, fills us with enthusiasm, and overcomes the fear of suffering in the pursuit of our desire. So, it is easy to see that desire and longing go together like identical twins. And in many cases, the object of our fierce desire may also be reflecting a secret yearning for something unrealized deep within our own makeup.

Spiritual growth and individuation are fueled by longings for love, safety, peace, wholeness, and meaning. And the more we are open to pursuing the journey that these longings can initiate, the more we can discover not only the increasing strength of our desire, passion, and creativity but also how much more we become engaged in our lives. Spirituality and individuation rest on the development of personal consciousness that comes from first being fully engaged in life and then reflecting upon our experiences. The vehicle of spiritual growth and individuation is the archetypal path of transformation, life, death, and rebirth.

The famous German literary figure Goethe beautifully sums up the points I'm trying to make in his poem "The Holy Longing." The poem goes like this:

> Tell a wise person, or else keep silent,
> Because the mass man will mock it right away.
> I praise what is truly alive,
> What longs to be burned to death.
>
> In the calm water of the love-nights,
> where you were begotten, where you have begotten,
> a strange feeling comes over you
> when you see the silent candle burning.
>
> Now you are no longer caught
> In the obsession with darkness,
> and a desire for higher love-making
> sweeps you upward.
>
> Distance does not make you falter.
> Now, arriving in magic, flying,
> and finally, insane for the light,
> you are the butterfly and you are gone.
> And so long as you haven't experienced this: to die and so to grow,
> you are only a troubled guest on the dark earth.

Johann Wolfgang von Goethe, "The Holy Longing"
Translated from the German by Robert Bly

Our Longings and Spiritual Life

Now, having finished my brief introduction on longing and the beautiful poem by Goethe, which I thought I understood for decades before I really did, I want to return to some more practical thoughts and recount how I found myself on this path.

Let me begin by asking you a few questions you have probably considered. Do you have trouble believing in God? Have you ever asked yourself what in the creeds, doctrines, or practices of your religious institutions makes any sense? Did you ever wonder how a God of love happened to create a world full of pain and evil? Well, during my mid-life quest I realized these questions had never bothered me very much. My focus had been on being furious with God.

My spiritual crisis began when I was ten years old and continued for another thirty plus years. It began when my mother was suffering from cancer and died a few years later. Suffering through this trauma in our family destroyed everything I had been taught in Sunday school and church. At ten years of age, I found no comfort in the religious platitudes I was offered and felt that the idea of a loving God was a lie. Of course, in the religion of my early life, there was no understanding that love must go beyond sentimentality and become the foundation of our being or that my entire life was supposed to be a spiritual journey with purpose and meaning. And the idea that I could find renewal and growth through my personal conflicts and suffering would have been considered scandalous in the church I attended as a child.

What I wasn't aware of at the time was that my early trauma was thrusting me into the front line of changing religious history. Of course, I stayed stuck in my anger with God and paid little attention to changing religious history or the more intellectual questions I mentioned earlier. The betrayal I experienced had seared my soul and dominated my religious perspectives.

Meanwhile, in the world outside of myself, it seemed clear that our religious institutions had been slipping into the neurosis of the modern age for the better part of the last two centuries. Now, when Jungians speak of neurosis, we mean that someone, or an institution, becomes increasingly one-sided, unbalanced, and cut off from their depths. As a neurosis grows, it is accompanied by a corresponding loss of meaning that brings on fear, anxiety, and regressions into the past. As the neurotic cycle between fear and defensiveness develops, the situation becomes worse. We all know that many of us have had disappointing, disillusioning, and even damaging experiences with our religious institutions. We can easily see the sexism, hypocrisy, literalism, power drives, sexual obsessions, and exclusivity in these establishments. Our psychological perspective can help us realize that all of these problems are symptoms of the old authoritative and easily understandable religious ways breaking down and calling for transformation.

But even more than this is going on here. Many of us feel betrayed as I did, and in fact we have been betrayed. Jung points out in his Commentary on *The Secret of the Golden Flower* that all of the great religions are meant to be therapies for the soul as it travels the difficult path of life. When they fail at this task, we feel betrayed, often angry and alienated, because we have lost our support—the value of a guiding myth as we travel through life. To make matters even more difficult, we are being called upon to treat the neurosis of our religious organizations and the pain they are inflicting upon us and our society.

As our institutions are floundering, regressing, and even growing in darker directions, we, as individuals, are called upon to carry the responsibility for our spiritual lives. This is a responsibility that our ancestors projected onto the church or temple—as many people still do or try to do. Far too many simply go into denial of the importance of their religious life or look for a new religion to project this responsibility onto.

The reality is that as we grow in consciousness and complexity, institutions can no longer carry this responsibility for us. And as we become more conscious, our longing for transformation and wholeness—in other words our Holy Longing—will become more pressing. From the Jungian standpoint, spirituality is an instinct and there is a religious function in our psyche. Denial or repression of this reality leads us to serve the idols of our neurosis, our culture, or to fill these needs with addictions. This perspective doesn't mean our institutions are no longer important or that they should be closed down. It means that the responsibility for our spiritual lives and for renewing our institutions is now ours, and we need to find a new model for our personal spiritual growth, for renewing our institutions, and for responding to our Holy Longing.

Holy Longing as Fundamental Aspect to our Nature

Before I go further in talking about how we can develop a new model, I want to say a few words about Jung, his work, and his intentions. After all, because he dared to talk openly about our religious and spiritual problems, he was criticized, it seems, by almost everyone under the sun. Because of these criticisms, I want to emphasize three important points here.

The first one is that Jung thought that if we lack a structure—a myth—with symbolic markers that guides us to stand in awe of something greater than ourselves and to serve it, then nature will rush in to fill this archetypal gap in our lives. This gap will be filled from our shadow, our woundedness, our anxiety, or some other deep place in our unconscious. Consequently, we will be diverted from living a creative, fulfilling, authentic life. And as Dr. Jung pointed out in his correspondence with Bill Wilson, cofounder of Alcoholics Anonymous, we will have no firm ground to stand upon in opposition to evil.

My second point is—and listen carefully because this is a very important point—the Jungian individuation process is not intended in any way to be a new religion. Jung meant the individuation process to be a way to reimagine the Christian myth, to revitalize and heal Christianity, and to have the same potential to help members of other religions find new purpose, meaning, and support for their lives in their own religions.

For my third point, I want to say that I believe that Jung was very clear in his thinking that both religion and spirituality are archetypally based. This means, in Jung's view, that they are fundamental aspects of our nature, and if we repress them, they will find energy in our shadows and become complexes.

Because religion is a function in our psychic makeup, we must respect it as a part of life. And when the institutions expressing the religious function are outgrown, they must be opened up and transformed carefully and consciously to meet the complexity and great needs in our world.

And in order to honor the power of spirituality, we must accept spirituality as being based on awe and "the idea of the holy," but we must also humanize the holy, personalize it, and find it within ourselves in a way that gives us a renewed sense of purpose, meaning, and hope as well as a love of life and others. Jung thought that religion needs spirituality for inspiration and transformation and that spirituality needs religion to give it form and grounding in our lives.

Our Longings for Wholeness

The next question I would like to approach is, how did I come across my own spiritual longings and a path that would satisfy them? Well, after being furious with God for a few decades, I found myself in Zurich, training to become an analyst and in analysis with Dr. John Mattern. One sunny afternoon, John quietly told me that anyone who was this mad with God must be in for a lifelong spiritual quest. I left that session and walked out into the park by Lake Zurich at the Stadelhofen train station, mad at John. But as the weeks went by, I began to realize that he might be right. At the same time, I was beginning to prepare for my upcoming comparative religions exams at the Jung Institute. As a background for these exams, I had to write a paper, and in the introduction to that paper, I examined my experiences of the mainstream religions I had known throughout my life. I reached three conclusions about them:

1. Many of the churches that I was familiar with had become professional organizations, and the workers in them were in reality pursuing careers. Transformation, which everyone seemed to assume happened when you joined the church or had a cathartic experience, rarely seemed to me to have taken place. In other words, church became something to attend and was professionally led and managed. In this setting religion became safe, and transformation is never safe. And while religious institutions offered biblical interpretations and doctrines, they did little to give me a vision of life or any practices to help me experience the truth of these doctrines or the reality of the deep eternal truths that the doctrines were supposed to represent.

2. A surprisingly large number of our churches were regressing into a fear-based fundamentalism, which is a full-force defense against the creative transformations brought on by a true experience of the Divine. Such churches have taken this position

54

out of self-interest, since they no longer have a trustworthy process to contain and guide this transformative process.

3. A new kind of church was rapidly emerging that focused on positive thinking and positive emotions as an approach to life. The appeal of these churches rests on the fact that what they present is compensatory to our longings and even to the depression and anxiety that is so prevalent in our society. Unfortunately, in the long run this approach fails to truly face and fulfill our longings and fails to transform our lives at a profound level.

Mysticism as Soul Force

These conclusions left me discouraged as to how to prepare the paper for my exam, because I wanted it to be personally relevant as well as academic. Then while reading Jung's last great book, *Mysterium Coniunctionis*, I came across the section where he describes mysticism as the "soul force" of religion. What Jung means here is that the mystics recognized their longing as a longing for wholeness and for transformation that would carry them deep into the relationship with the Divine. Throughout history, the mystics have carried the mysteries of transformation, which can return creativity to religion and transform it into a spiritual quest. The mystic vision arises out of the great religions and becomes critical of their institutions when their dogma has rigidified. The mystics replace fear with awe, authority with compassion, and duty with love. They reclaim the true purpose of dogma, which is to channel our relationship to the numinous, to support and liberate spiritual growth—not limit it.

Like that of the mystics, much of Carl Jung's mission in life was to free religion and spiritual consciousness from their self-imposed shackles and to free our hearts to accept our deepest longing. Mysticism breaks the mold of our approach to religion and returns us to the ground or source of our being—and our capacity to experience and relate to the Divine, which means to life, from our hearts. The faith of the mystics was not a belief in creedal doctrines—and once again I invite you to listen carefully because this is a very important point—faith for the mystics is a sense of trust and loyalty in the results of the process of spiritual development that they had worked out. In this process one learns to know and trust God through the pursuit of self-knowledge, because this pursuit ultimately reveals that something transcendent is working in our lives and that our devotion to discovering, understanding, and co-creating with this force will continually transform our lives in a surprising way.

Unfortunately the religions I experienced earlier in my life had forgotten mysticism and, therefore, the profound aspects of spirituality and transformation. The mystical process has been left back in the Middle Ages and shows up only in religious history books. This process has not been re-imagined into our times. Dr. Jung undertook this re-imagining because he saw the Holy Longing—the longing for transformation and wholeness—first in himself and then in his many patients.

For the working title of the paper for my exam, I chose "Fire in the Soul" because it reflected how deeply this subject moved me. In my paper, I compared the mystical process as presented by the great Anglican scholar Evelyn Underhill in her landmark book, *Mysticism: The Nature and Development of Spiritual Consciousness,* with Jung's individuation process and with the Lakota vision quest, because I wanted to include the archetypal structure of a natural religion.

In preparing for this exam, I realized that Jung had taken the perennial path of the mystics in all of the great religions out of the Middle Ages and re-imagined this path into a system of growth, healing, and wholeness that has its context and meanings grounded in the experiences of my times. His individuation process then becomes one of the most profound experiences and ways of life that we can encounter.

Therefore, individuation can become the vehicle for moving us from a belief-based religion to a practice-based religion, using practices that honor our traditions and yet are on the cutting edge of spiritual and psychological growth. And as these practices lead us into self-knowledge, we also discover the presence of the Divine in our lives, the depths of our longings, and their fulfillment.

Questions to Expand Our Understanding

As I was talking about our many levels of longing, the neurosis of religion in modern times, some of Jung's perspectives, and my journey, what kinds of thoughts, memories, and questions came to mind for you?

Steps on the Mystic's Path and the Individuation Process

In this section of the lecture, I am going to focus on the steps on the mystic's path and the developmental phases of the individuation process, which can aid us in constructing a new model for our personal spiritual growth and for renewing our institutions.

In our current world, we are so out of touch with the meaning of mysticism that we often think of it as a New Age, airy-fairy activity that isn't grounded in reality. In fact, just the opposite is true. The mystical path is a practical, grounded, psychologically sophisticated series of steps that are meant to lead the human soul into the realization of a greater sense of reality, higher consciousness, and a life in harmony with the Divine—however you choose to understand that term.

The mystics and Jung face three important psycho-spiritual facts:

1. Spirituality is transformation. Jung points out that transformation—life, death, and rebirth—is the symbolic description of how we grow. The mystics had naturally incorporated this pattern into their process and recognized it as the Divine pattern of growth.

2. Inner work, pursuing the inner journey—if it is real and transformative—is never just about you. To begin with, being fully engaged in life requires other people. We must have relationships—which entail not only love and friendships but also conflicts, disappointments, and most of all projections—to fully learn about ourselves. Then as we grow, our growth benefits the people around us. It saves them from the projections and influence of our shadows and we all become enlivened. The journey leads us into a more creative life. We become cocreators with the Self or the Divine, and we have a positive influence in the world.

Suffering is not a [?] of defeat in character [?] sign of defeat in character

3. The mystics and Jung accept is that life is difficult. We must accept this fact and be able to see beyond our illusionary fantasies of life—goals of fun, happiness, and abundance or even a "good life"—in order to become open first to true suffering and then to true joy, inspiration, and hope.

As I was reflecting on having put these three facts together in my paper and on John's comment to me about accepting that my life should become a spiritual quest, I realized that I was experiencing an awakening—the realization of a new perspective on myself and about my life.

Awakening is the first step on the mystic's path. But I found this realization a bit strange. I thought I had already awakened. After all, I had been on the inner journey for a long time. I hadn't realized, however, that awakening is also part of the archetypal pattern of growth, and we must experience awakening again and again, every time we start a new cycle of transformation. Initially, we must begin to awaken from the trance of our conventional life and how we were taught to adapt to it. While we are in this trance, we share the thoughts that we know who we really are, that we are able to make conscious choices, and that we understand the complexities of the issues facing us. We continue to make erroneous, even destructive choices and devote our life's energies to things that are depleting us rather than supporting us. We do this because we fail to realize that we are looking at life through the lens of our adaptive identity and our personal and cultural complexes.

Awakening from this trance—and remember we must awaken again and again—means seeing and hearing the truth of our own reality. This can come only through developing consciousness through self-knowledge within the context of what I call the Soul Contract.

The Soul Contract begins with our becoming fully engaged in life and proceeds as we learn a disciplined practice of reflecting upon our experiences until our reflections enlarge or transform our consciousness; we integrate this new level of consciousness into our lives. If the process doesn't change how we are living and how we are spending our energy, then no transformation has taken place. Attending to the Soul Contract builds our ability to see the world and life differently

58

and, ultimately, to see the deeper reality that is reflected in all life.

It is reflecting upon our experiences that brings self-knowledge and increasing consciousness to us. Saint Catherine of Siena says that self-knowledge is the only true path to God. Saint Teresa of Ávila has this to say about self-knowledge:

> Self-knowledge is so important that I do not care how high you are raised up to the heavens. I never want you to cease cultivating it...Enter the room of self-knowledge first, instead of floating off to other places. This is the path. Traveling along a safe and level road, who needs wings to fly? Let's make the best possible use of our feet first and learn to know ourselves.

Dr. Jung would certainly agree with these two mystics, who were made doctors of the church for their great intellectual contributions to religious life. There is a great poignancy for me when I talk about self-knowledge in a spiritual context. Not too long ago I had a dream in which the Presbyterian pastor from my childhood was standing at a table in the back of the church I now attend. He was very old. As I walked up to him, tears filled my eyes. I was thinking to myself as I hugged him that this is the man who baptized me and buried my mother. Then I realized he was raising money for foreign missions—something I don't believe in when the missions are focused on conversions. And I was filled with a deep sense of sadness in the dream. What fills me with sadness in reality is that the people in that church were not malicious, they were unconscious.

And this sadness reminds me of the statement the twentieth century theologian Reinhold Niebuhr made that "most evil is not done by evil people, but by good people who don't know what they are doing." Many of you have heard me quote Niebuhr before, and I continue to do so because it is incredibly sad to me to see how much of the sorrow in our lives happens because we or other people were too threatened to really look inside themselves and at the deeper reality of our lives.

Perhaps, however, our greatest hope comes from the fact, according to Evelyn Underhill, that the creative spirit of the Divine is always seeking to shape our lives as a journey of personal transformation. In the individuation process, life is a journey of personal transformations that are archetypically structured in our psyche. "The worst of it all," Jung writes, "is that intelligent and cultivated people live their lives without even knowing of the possibility of such transformations." He continues, "Thoroughly unprepared, we take the step into the afternoon of life. Worse still we take this step with the false assumption that our truths and ideals will serve us as they did in the past." But what was great in the past won't work in the future. Either a personal crisis or a general feeling of dissatisfaction will usher in the call that our unconscious or spiritual energy is surging, seeking recognition and wholeness through transformation. The call and awakening are the first steps on a journey that is mapped by both Jung and the mystics.

In our transformative model of spiritual and psychological development, we have seen that awakening, usually due to a call, is the first phase. If we answer the call, we will begin to seek self-knowledge in a phase the mystics called purification; Jungians term this "the realization of the shadow." I call it the descent into life, and you can soon see how counter cultural this part of the journey is.

I always find it interesting, even amusing, that when the newest pied piper for enlightenment is speaking in town, he or she is usually focusing on how we can achieve peace and joy. Well, no wonder! That is what sells or what creates followings, because that is what so many of us think we are longing for.

On the other hand, all of our great religions (and I am not speaking of the pied pipers they also have)—those religions that the religious scholar Huston Smith calls our wisdom traditions—have a very different emphasis. For example, a rabbi famous in Jewish history lived in a tent pitched next to the walls of Jerusalem, because he wanted to be close to the poor. Prince Siddhartha walked out of his father's palace and came face to face with poverty, illness, and death; and these encounters began his journey into becoming the Buddha. In Christianity, the Gospel of Matthew says that when Jesus was questioned about the people he liked to spend his time with, he replied, "For I have come to call not the righteous but sinners."

Our spiritual traditions tell us that the root meaning of the word *salvation* is "the way of redemption" or "the way to wholeness." As we follow this line of thinking, we discover that our journey into wholeness (or holiness, in the words of the mystical traditions) begins in a paradoxical way—not by a search for peace and joy but by acknowledging the grit and grist of life: suffering, illness, death, and our alienation from ourselves and the depth of our own spiritual and psychological capacities. Now, this is a very important point: It is the full acceptance of these aspects of ourselves that initiates our journey into becoming fully human, fully incarnated, and more open to love and joy.

Of course, we all want a good life. And when we encounter life's difficulties, we want peace of mind and good relationships, and we want to keep our lifestyle and habits—the selves we are used to. And of course, our culture supports this point of view. The culture doesn't see our wounds and difficulties as calls for transformation. It sees them as symptoms to alleviate so we can get back to "normal," which actually means "functional in a social way," not a spiritual, psychological, or even personally fulfilling way.

In addition, most of us want to have a vision of a successful, prosperous, and fulfilling life; and if we have children, we want to have a dream of a successful life for them. We get angry with them, ourselves, and life when our dreams and visions fail. But the failures of these dreams and visions are very important, for they are meant to awaken us to compassion—compassion not for others, but for ourselves and for how difficult life is.

Generally we need our dreams of a good life to carry us into adulthood. But later, we also need for these dreams to fail, in order to make way for our wholeness to begin to emerge and be discovered. And we need the self-compassion these experiences can generate, in order to accept the difficulties in our lives as spiritual and psychological incubations and not as failures. Plus, as we begin to do the work in what Jung called "the realization of our shadow," we need this capacity for compassion in order to accept the poor, dispossessed, and disapproved parts of ourselves.

To illustrate this point, I'll share with you the words of the Ba'al Shem Tov, founder of the Hassidic tradition in Judaism. He said,

61

"There are many rooms in God's house." Does that sound familiar? He then went on to say, "There is, however, one key that opens every room, and that key is a broken heart." The statement of the Ba'al Shem Tov reminds us of the emotional reality involved in the realization of our shadow, in making a true descent into life. But why, we might ask ourselves, is this statement true?

The answer is that as we formed our identities, we generally identified with characteristics, feelings, ideas, and attitudes that we felt would make our lives work, and these qualities came to represent what we thought were our strengths and best values. In other words, we developed our own unconscious lists of virtues and vices to guide us. When these identifications begin to fail, people come in to see us professionally, because they have become unhappy or discontented or were never able to form a workable list and want their suffering to stop. Two things make it possible for our suffering to begin to stop: First is the acceptance of our suffering—remember self-compassion is needed, not self-judgment. According to Jung, acceptance is the necessary first step in transforming anything psychological. But our next question is, what will our suffering be transformed into? The answer, according to Jung, is not into peace and joy but into true suffering, which means facing the early wounds within ourselves and the truth of our inner contradictions.

The second thing we must do is value the inhabitants of our shadows—the parts of ourselves that have been disowned, devalued, rejected, and repressed. This all starts with some of our most negative feelings and self-critical voices.

Let me read you a piece from the *New York Times* article on *The Red Book* that explains what I mean.

> Creating the book also led Jung to reformulate how he worked with clients, as evidenced by an entry the editor and translator, Shamdasani, found in a self-published book written by a former client, in which she recalls Jung's advice for processing what went on in the deeper and sometimes frightening parts of her mind.

"I should advise you to put it all down as beautifully as you can—in some beautifully bound book," Jung instructed. "It will seem as if you were making the visions banal—but then you need to do that—then you are freed from the power of them…Then when these things are in some precious book you can go to the book and turn over the pages and for you it will be your church—your cathedral—the silent places of your spirit where you will find renewal. If anyone tells you that it is morbid or neurotic and you listen to them—then you will lose your soul—for in that book is your soul."

This is the way my wife, Massimilla, and I value our own shadows. You might also want to remember that nothing in our shadow frightens us more than our own denied and impoverished potentials.

Getting to Know Our Shadows

Getting to know our shadows is a painful journey because we must crucify our own good opinions of ourselves. The mystics aptly termed this process the "purification of the self." Literature and mythology refer to this process as a "descent" that requires trust, courage, and usually a guide. And as is the case with awakening, we find that each transformation involves a new realization of a part of our shadow.

One of the greatest things we learn from the realization of our shadow is self-compassion, and this is truly the answer to one of our greatest, but rarely admitted, longings. Moreover, self-compassion is the necessary foundation for being truly compassionate with others and for being able to accept the idea of Divine compassion personally.

We also learn that our ego is a vitally important part of our personality. In this process with our shadow, the ego becomes both smaller and stronger and begins to realize it must serve something greater than it is: either the Self or the Divine.

In addition, because this work involves dreams, symbols, and metaphors, which we will discuss further tomorrow, we begin to see what Jung meant by the importance of the symbolic life. Religion, life, and oneself can only be wholly understood through the use of metaphor and symbol, as we have seen in our use of the word shadow. Love, life, spirituality—all have a mysterious foundation that can be seen only through symbol and metaphor.

Working with our shadows makes the archetypal pattern of transformation a very personal experience. In the pattern of life, death, and rebirth, we experience the death aspect as tension, betrayal, conflict, and destruction—tension between our deep values and conventional values or obligations, conflict within ourselves and with others over these tensions, and the destruction of our fantasies and ideas of how things should be or what we want, for example.

The simple reality is that psycho-spiritual growth means we must be willing to dissolve our old personalities, our conventional selves—the identities we formed unconsciously, for the most part—in our search for wholeness and the fullness in life that will honor our longings. Paradoxically, the journey that leads us to this act or experience simultaneously brings us to the realization of our true selves. Here we are encountering one of the great truths in life. Dissolution is also creation. The path of transformation is life, death, and rebirth—creation comes from the conflict and destruction taking place in a strongly lived life—and each transformation takes us closer to our spiritual goal, which is to become fully human.

Let me share another personal example with you. A few decades ago, when I was changing careers from business to psychology, I had a dream that illustrated the conflict I was experiencing. I wanted to pursue a new life—in fact, I believed that my life depended upon this pursuit, which required me to go back to graduate school. Yet I also had children. I greatly valued them and the quality of their lives, which also meant I still had to earn a living. In the midst of this conflict, I dreamed I was on a cross. Below me, on my right, was a group of older people, representing traditional values, looking up at me. On my left was a group of children, representing the future, also looking up at me. For the children's sake, I—that is my ego, my sense of identity—was going to have to die and be reborn with a perspective that was broad enough and a heart that was big enough to hold the tensions of this conflict and carry it into the future.

Now once again listen carefully, because this is a very important point. True peace and peace brought on by wisdom in the individuation process is the acceptance of tension, betrayal, and conflict as signs of the Divine presence or the Self at work. The nature of the Divine and the Self is creativity, and it is creativity that overcomes death. True peace, a longing we all share, comes from accepting this reality. And this knowledge also helps us understand why Jung says, "The love of God can be terrible," and what the mystics mean by *illumination*.

Illumination is constantly talked about by teachers, gurus, and seekers. But illumination or the illuminative way comes only through the self-knowledge gained from the realization of our shadows. This is the only kind of work that leads us to be aware of ourselves as separate from the forces that molded us. And it is only this work that shows us we are not unique personalities unless we have made this separation and have come into an ongoing deeper relationship with ourselves and all life.

The journey of individuation as a spiritual model brings us into the new state of consciousness that the mystics called the illuminative way. As I have said, attaining this state begins with knowing our shadow, which includes our repressed emotional and instinctual potential for vitality. The illuminative way is the first step in releasing our longing to live a passionate life. While our journey progresses, our perspective transforms, and as we go up the spiral staircase of developing consciousness, we understand the necessity of living wholeheartedly. *It is our wholehearted engagement with our inner and outer lives that gives us the food for our reflections.* This is what I refer to as our Soul Contract because of the importance of realizing that we cannot obtain the knowledge beforehand; that can come only as the result of being committed to a full engagement in life.

Many of you know that one of my favorite stories from Jung supports this point. When Jung is talking about Saul's conversion to Paul in the New Testament, he says, "Saul owed his conversion neither to true love, nor to true faith, nor to any other truth. It was solely his hatred of the Christians that set him on the road to Damascus and to that decisive experience which was to alter the whole course of his life. He was brought to this experience by following out, with conviction his own worst mistake." In another place, Jung uses this story to illustrate the point that if we pursue the wrong thing with all of our heart, we will end up at the right place.

In the illuminative way of consciousness in individuation, we realize the answer to Martin Buber's question: "Can you teach me to have faith in reality, in the truth of our existence?" We are now learning to see reality and our existence truthfully. We are able to commit to the beauty of life as it is, including our mistakes, without the crippling self-judgment of conventional perspectives. The awareness of ourselves as separate from the forces that molded us and our adoptive identities invites us into the experiences of personal authenticity and of feeling at home within ourselves—another secret longing we all share, which is part of our Holy Longing.

The spiritual and psychological growth needed to sustain a life of transformation has always required methodical devotion and practices. If we want a life with meaning, fulfillment, joy, love, and purpose, we have to pay attention to it. These are the fruits of self-knowledge and spiritual development and cannot be gained any other way. Whatever illusion or defense we distract ourselves with—whether it is busyness, obligations, or being a pleaser, achiever, or whatever—it is a defensive excuse for avoiding the dangers of transformation and for losing the benefits that transformation offers.

If, however, we begin to keep a journal, write down our dreams, and do active imagination, several interesting things will happen. We will begin to think in terms of reflecting on our lives or losing them. Just the act of being there for our soul becomes powerful and life-enhancing. The more we examine our lives, the more natural it becomes to see the world in symbolic terms and to realize that the capacity for symbolic vision is the foundation of a conscious and spiritual life. It becomes apparent that if our holy books are not seen through the eyes of metaphor, they become ridiculous and contradictory and lose their ability to inform our lives. And we are led to realize that paying attention is the acid test of love, and we must love ourselves and life in this most important way.

And finally a few words about the unitive way, or the experience of wholeness. As I said earlier, when we examine the root meanings of the word *salvation*, which we hear so often in religious circles, we find that it means "to become intact." Salvation is the way to redemption and the way to wholeness. In individuation and mysticism, the path is the way to wholeness, and the process itself engenders love. As we look at the contribution of Underhill, we see that the mystics considered the unitive life to be one that reflected a unification of the personality on high levels and that perceived reality with clarity and awareness of its profound implications. And ecstasy, according to Underhill, is simply the experience of unity and wholeness.

The individuation process—consciously being in life in relationship to our greater Self—leads to a constantly evolving and deepening "I and Thou" relationship with our center. Our greater Self, or the Divine presence within, is an inner companion that teaches, heals, and centers our development. As we detect this presence and realize that it is the One guiding our particular strand into the web of life, the perspective we have on our life story changes dramatically.

Consciousness brings our greatest healing as it links our minds, bodies, emotions, and spirit into one focused whole. Through consciousness, we discover the Self: the Divine within that infuses our bodies, minds, and hearts with life, love, and creative power and allows us to understand the underlying notion of wholeness that the great religions all suggest.

To feel the sense of wholeness supporting life is like coming home to ourselves. It is a moment of joy and serenity. And while it's a moment we can enjoy, it's not one we can hold on to. If we try, the effort will imprison us in the same way that never wanting to leave home can prevent our journey from continuing. You see, the unitive life is not the top of the spiral staircase. It is a new landing on the staircase. But life as a dynamic force goes on, and we are called to meet new situations, to be creative in new ways, to grow again, to continue the steps of the process toward a new level with another landing. In this process we have the opportunity to accumulate the riches of a growing soul—a soul that permeates and enlarges our personality—which becomes an

67

abundant personality in which courage, generosity, compassion, joy, and love come naturally.

The old religion I grew up in amplified my failings and impoverishment that came from simply being a human being. Atonement was misunderstood in this religious perspective as being a denial of self through service, instead of a journey inward that opens us to the inspiration, creativity, and joy that create a life being lived as a service to life, in its greater sense.

It is important to know and heal our wounds, to know our inhibitions and complexes, and to have walked through our own darkness. We must also be able to understand and accept the story of our suffering and misfortunes. Knowing all of this has several great purposes. First, this wisdom opens us to compassion and the ability to love. Then, the realization of our shadow leads us to be open to our strengths, visions, creativity, hope, and joy. This is the journey that opens us to knowledge of the Divine working in our lives and to the experience of being carried through life and sustained. And we are able to experience our deepest sense of personal existence by forgetting ourselves—rather than by fighting for ourselves or, as in most cases, fighting with ourselves.

I would like to close by sharing an excerpt from Friedrich Schiller's poem "Ode to Joy " which as you may know provided the words to the final movement of Beethoven's Ninth Symphony:

> Joy, beautiful spark of Gods,
> Daughter of Elysium,
> We approach, fueled by fire,
> Heavenly, your sanctuary,
> Your magical power unify
> What custom harshly parts
> All men are made brothers
> Where your gentle wing spreads.
> Those who dwell in the great circle,
> Render homage unto compassion!
> It guides us to the stars,
> Where the Unknown reigns.

Questions to Expand Our Understanding

1. I would like to ask you for your questions, comments, and reactions.

2. Did anything surprise you in this section?

3. Do you have any reflections on Saul's conversion to Paul?

Chapter 4 : Seminar

FIRE IN THE SOUL:
A Jungian Guide to Discovering the Promise
in Our Holy Longing

I have mentioned that most of us don't feel compelled to look into life's bigger questions unless we have a traumatic history or feel like our life isn't working. Or perhaps the bottom falls out, and we are face-to-face with the big questions: Who am I? Why am I here? What can this all mean? Then we begin longing for answers, while at the same time, in many cases, we are trying to defend ourselves against our longings and our fears.

In the area of religion, I noted that Jung was well acquainted with the longings of the human heart that Martin Buber articulated as questions to religion: "Can you teach me to have faith in reality, in the truth of our existence, so that my life will have purpose, meaning, and a way of being fulfilled?" This question expresses a very sophisticated kind of longing.

Then I went on to mention that the Jungian analyst Dr. James Hillman takes our longings to the most basic level. Some examples are "Help! Please help me," or "Take me, just as I am, no judgments, no questions asked," or "Take me without my having to do something, or be someone," or the cry, "Hold me," or "Don't go away; never leave me alone." These pleas may be saying, "Love me," or "Teach me, guide me, show me what to do, or tell me how." And sometimes we hear the hopelessness in a soul that says, "Leave me alone. Just let me be."

These longings range from the primitive child, the symbol of our eternal vulnerability, to the sophisticated longings articulated by Martin Buber. It is also important to note that this same child archetype within us is also pointing us toward our future.

Questions for Reflection

Now I would like you to sit back for just a minute, close your eyes, and ask yourself these questions:

1. How conscious are you of your longings?
2. What kinds of emotions do they bring up in you?
3. Where do you feel these emotions in your body?
4. How do you nurture, love, honor, and care for your longings?

These are important questions; take about five minutes and write your responses to them. Include the feelings, images, and thoughts that come up in you.

I'm sure you've figured out that I just asked you to do a counter cultural activity. We are supposed to focus on goals, accomplishing things, being independent, paying attention to other people, positive thinking, and so on. I'll say more about that, but I want to emphasize that our deepest longings make up the deepest core of what it means to be human. These longings will consciously or unconsciously affect our journey into the future.

In the lecture, I shared how the trauma of my early life alienated me from religion and how I rediscovered a connection with my religious and spiritual selves while I was training in Zurich. Due to trauma and the historical period I was in, I lost my sense of "religio"—my link with the source of my being and all being. The first thing I had to recognize was that I needed to acknowledge the yearning for this link in myself, which wasn't easy. You may remember that I told you that I became mad with my analyst when he told me that anyone who was as mad at God as I was, and had been for decades, was in for a lifelong spiritual quest. My recognition of the need for "religio" also meant accepting my lack of spiritual resources—my inability to truly feed myself spiritually and to be engaged in life spiritually.

By recognizing this need for "religio," we acknowledge how abandoned by and disconnected from our institutional religions we have been. As these institutions have failed to re-imagine their messages and practices into the current age, they have betrayed us, and we, paradoxically, are left with the responsibility for transforming them.

When we have lost our connection with our soul, when our Self is silent, when our center is empty and we have no vital mythic structure for reconnecting to it, we easily fall prey to the common sense, conventional wisdom around us. This voice tells us to do "what anybody in his right mind would do"—to hold tightly to conventional values and not to do anything extreme. In this situation our Holy Longing, which is generally denied and repressed, gathers power in our shadows. Then instead of trying to awaken to our calls for transformation—our unhappiness, symptoms, and even illnesses—we try to overcome them. Even our psychological and spiritual practices are actually geared toward having a big, strong, goal-directed, enlightened ego. The term *self-actualization* actually plays right into this common mistake. Even people in analysis, pursuing esoteric and religious paths, often flounder because they are trying to attain wholeness, balance, or enlightenment with their egos. They have little idea of what really needs to be sacrificed here and how the ego needs to be transformed.

I also talked about my experience of discovering a new model for my spirituality, which in a general sense was grounded in the traditional wisdom of the major religions, and this model is based on the path of mysticism. I also explained how our institutions have lost the knowledge of that path because they left it in the language of the Middle Ages in religious history books. Dr. Jung, however, took this knowledge very seriously and re-imagined it into his individuation process, which gives us the knowledge and practices that can enliven our religious and spiritual lives and our traditions, as well as bring healing and wholeness into our lives.

It is fundamental on both the mystical path and the path of individuation to understand the following statements. First, if we are in some sense unique creations and there is a possibility of a divine spark within us, or a deeper Self that defines the essence of each one

of us, then self-knowledge is the only way to develop ongoing transformational knowledge. And self-knowledge entails a great deal more
than simply noting our moods, emotions, memories, thoughts, and
behaviors and trying to accept or correct them. Second, if each one
of us is part of the world soul—the collective unconscious or the divine nature—then self-knowledge becomes the way to learn about the
trustworthy reality Martin Buber is talking about: the longed for hopes
and dreams of our soul. Self-knowledge becomes the vehicle and force
for inner self-creation, by which our evolving personality transforms,
lives, dies, and is reborn as a more comprehensive version of ourselves,
meaning we become more of what we are meant to be.

Individuation gives us a new perspective, a new language, and new
practices to help us understand the experiences that are granted to all
of us as human beings. These are the experiences of a life in which we
are fully engaged, and they are ones that need to be cultivated and reflected upon, intentionally and precisely, in order to serve as a force not
only for self-knowledge but also for self-transformation. Individuation
invites this process into our lives.

Questions to Expand Our Understanding

Now I have presented some more fairly intense ideas to you. I want you
to take a moment, maybe take a deep breath, then journal some of your
thoughts.

1. Did anything I said make you feel uncomfortable?
2. Did anything make you feel engaged or energized?
3. Were you surprised at any point?

Awakening

Next, I would like to review what I said about awakening, because
awakening is the first step on all mystical paths and on any path leading
to transformation and consciousness. I shared that while I was working
on my paper for the comparative religions exam at the Jung Institute,
and trying to digest my analyst's comment that I should accept the fact
that my life was meant to be a spiritual quest, I realized that I was expe-

riencing an awakening—the realization of a new perspective on myself and about my life. But I found this realization a bit strange. I thought I had already awakened. After all, I had been on the inner journey for a long time. However, I hadn't realized that awakening is also part of the archetypal pattern of growth and that we must experience awakening again and again, every time we start a new cycle of transformation.

Initially we must awaken from the trance of our conventional life and how we learned to adapt to it. While we are in this trance, we share the illusion that we know who we really are, that we are able to make conscious choices, and that we understand the complexities facing us. In the unconsciousness of this position, we continue to make erroneous, even destructive choices and devote our life's energies to things that are depleting us rather than supporting us. We do this because we fail to realize that we are looking at life through the lens of our adaptive identity and our personal and cultural complexes. Complex driven

Awakening from this trance—and remember we must awaken again and again—means really seeing and hearing the truth about our own reality. This kind of self-awareness can come only through developing consciousness within the context of what I call the Soul Contract.

The Soul Contract begins with our becoming fully engaged in life and proceeds as we learn a disciplined practice of reflecting upon our experiences until our reflections enlarge and transform our consciousness and we integrate this new level of consciousness into our lives. If this process doesn't change how we are living and how we are spending our energy, then no transformation has taken place. Following the Soul Contract builds our ability to see the world and enables us to live differently and, ultimately, to see the deeper reality that is reflected in all life.

Awakening is usually preceded by a call, and these two things travel hand in hand. We have to ask ourselves why awakening is so problematic for most of us. The answer may be fear of a number of things. But it may also be that awakening and answering a call require a definite and ongoing focus of our energy. And we have difficulty focusing our energy on something that may become a crossroads in our lives.

In terms of attention and energy, we are usually swallowed by the streams of jobs, families, busyness, obligations, and even the nervous activities we pursue to please others or avoid conflicts. In addition, our energy is often devoured by our emotional reactions, our fears and desire, our pleasures and pains, our daydreams, and our imaginary worries. And in reality, when we are swallowed and devoured in this way, we no longer exist as an "I"—a true individual. We are not living our lives. They are living us, and the great danger is that we may eventually die without having awakened to what we really are—without having truly lived.

Questions for Reflection

Now I would like to ask you to make some of these ideas more personal. Read this quote from *Sacred Selfishness* (p. 298) about awakening to life and take time to journal your reflections and answer the questions that follow.

Moving through individuation as a quest for self-knowledge becomes a process of revealing to ourselves who we really are. The revelation follows a gradual process, punctuated by startling recognitions that move us toward a deeper sense of our true identities and the possibilities inherent in them.

1. What kinds of feelings came up in you?
2. Were any of you surprised?

The Struggle and The Shadow

It becomes easy to see that initially, most of us are not free enough or conscious enough to individuate without struggle and sacrifice. And all too often we gain a feeling of relief when we let our attention become absorbed again by the flow of a busy or a good life. Frequently we are restricted by our sense of duty and responsibility. Common sense warns us not to break the rules. We are too "good" in the conventional sense to individuate, which means we are too bound up by unspoken rules and regulations that are often, in fact, products of our own ideals and self-definition. Our parental complexes also threaten us with guilt, shame, and punishment if we even think of delving deeply and genuinely into our own inner lives, because this work will force us to change our values.

All of the things I've mentioned are threatening to our ego, which means our sense of who we are and our emotional safety. But our struggles with these things and how they affect us strengthen our ego and,

76

seemingly paradoxically, make the ego smaller and ready to serve the Self, the essence of who we can become.

Three qualities will emerge from this struggle, which we call the confrontation with the shadow. First is our ability to work through and assimilate our parental complexes, as well as the complexes of our culture. Working through both is necessary in order to develop an on-going relationship with the Self or with the Divine. Second is learning to trust the Self for our basic survival, which will give us the strength to sacrifice our ease and comfort and risk making sacrifices that violate the rules of common sense. Third is developing the ability to respond with love and desire to an image of our soul that we discover in a dream or active imagination. This ability allows us to make a full-hearted response to beauty, to the soul, to the other within us that completes us; such an experience of love breaks the shell of egohood and everyday life or everyday reality.

It is then, in the confrontation with our shadows—the process of purification, in the language of the mystics—that the greatest part of our work is done. And every step up on the spiral staircase of transformation will require that we confront a new piece of our shadow. Now, let me pose a question, because this is a very important point: Do you have an idea why this is true—that the more light we create, the more shadow comes into being?

Confronting Our Shadows

Before I address how to work with our shadows, I want to present and discuss two things that we must consider in order to develop the foundation necessary for realizing shadow material. The first one is the evolution of the Protestant ethic into a cultural complex that we have to deal with, and the second one is the set of important psycho-spiritual facts that Jung and the mystics shared.

Protestant Ethic as Cultural Complex

There is one major impediment that most of us face when we begin doing our inner work and especially work on our shadows. We share what I call our John Calvin complex, which is a complex in our cultural unconscious. Calvinism was originally brought to this country by the white settlers in New England. The writer Barbara Ehrenreich describes Calvinism as socially imposed depression. Calvinism spread from a narrow religion into a social ethic: the Protestant ethic. This ethic permeated our country and has become structured into our psyche, no matter what religion we actually belonged to.

In this ethic or religion, our task was to constantly examine "the loathsome abominations that lie in our bosom," and thereby seek to uproot the sinful thoughts that are a sure sign of damnation. And Calvinism offered only one relief from this anxiety-producing work of self-examination, and that was another form of labor: work, work, work. Idleness and pleasure-seeking were contemptible sins. This line of thinking morphed into a hellfire-and-damnation kind of fundamentalism that I can remember from my childhood. Drinking, dancing, and even fishing on Sunday could send you to hell.

Even if we do not personally believe anything like this, these views present a problem for us: We have been born into a notion that to reflect or look inside of ourselves means to do so in a self-critical, self-judgmental, condemning manner. We possess no ingrained notion to look into ourselves with compassion, love, inspiration, and hope. Even our helping professions are looking for things that are bad—now spoken of as dysfunctional—and how to correct them, not how to find transformation in them.

Now, to take this line of thinking a step further, it isn't hard to see how very critical we can be of ourselves, and we naturally seek relief by being busy, busy, busy. In fact, Barbara Ehrenreich reminds us in her book *Bright-Sided: How the Relentless Promotion of Positive Thinking Has Undermined America* that busyness for its own sake became a mark of status in the 1980s.

We all live in a country where this punitive ideology with its demand for perpetual effort and self-examination to the point of self-loathing is in our blood. And to make matters worse, our powerful advertising strategists and even our self-help gurus have learned how to take full advantage of this ideology and perpetuate it because it sells their products.

Now once again, I would like for you to sit back, take a deep breath, and think about what I have said. What kinds of thoughts, feelings, and images are coming up for you? It has taken me decades in my own work to root out how powerfully this complex affected me and to understand how difficult it is for me to be on the inner journey without looking for something to fix, defeat, or criticize. What we find inside, even if they are negative feelings, are symbolic, and they are like the frogs, loathly damsels, ogres, and giants in fairy tales—they are looking for transformation.

In his *Letters to a Young Poet*, Rilke beautifully sums up the paradoxes within our shadows and reverses the Protestant ethic by saying, "Perhaps all the dragons of our lives are princesses who are only waiting to see us once beautiful and brave. Perhaps everything terrible is in its deepest being something that needs our love."

As we proceed into the next section on confronting our shadows, I want to invite you to join me in looking at how our shadows hold our potentials while reflecting many of the paradoxes we live in and how our shadows help us challenge ourselves to new growth and meaning.

Important Psycho-Spiritual Facts

As background information for having the foundation to work with shadow material, I want to present to you the second thing I mentioned, which is the set of important psycho-spiritual facts that Jung and the mystics shared. These three psycho-spiritual facts are particularly important because they are the source of a lot of misunderstanding, criticism, and resistance—both inner and outer—that we will encounter on the journey.

1. In all of the mystical traditions, spirituality is transformation. And Jung points out that transformation—life, death, and rebirth—is the symbolic description of how we grow. The mystics had naturally incorporated this pattern into their process and recognized it as the Divine pattern of growth. So, spirituality equals transformation. In reality, this means that conflict, tension, betrayal, and trauma strike the fire in the soul that eventually burns away our old lives so that new ones may arise from the

79

ashes, like the phoenix. This is the image of spiritual and psychological transformation. And true peace in our hearts comes from accepting this process and opening ourselves to its benefits.

2. Inner work—pursuing the inner journey, if it is real and transformative—is never just about you. To begin with, being fully engaged in life requires other people. We must have relationships—with their love, friendships, conflicts, betrayals, disappointments, and, most of all, projections—in order to learn about ourselves. Then, as we grow, our growth benefits the people around us. It saves them from the projections and influences of our shadows and complexes, and then we all become enlivened. The journey leads us into a more creative life as we become co-creators with the Self or the Divine, enabling us to enrich the life of the world.

3. Life is difficult. In order to truly grow and transform, we must accept this fact and see beyond our illusionary fantasies of life—having goals of happiness, fun, and abundance or even there being a "good life"—in order to become open to true joy, inspiration, and hope.

The Descent Into Life

Well, now we are finally able to begin to talk about the realization of our shadow and the different complexes in it. As mentioned, I call this process the descent into life. I also shared that all of our great religions—or as the scholar Huston Smith calls them, our great wisdom traditions—have said all along that our journey into holiness or wholeness begins in a paradoxical way, not by a search for peace and joy but by acknowledging the grit and grist of life: suffering, illness, death, and our alienation from ourselves and the depth of our own spiritual and psychological capacities. Now, this is a very important point: It is the full acceptance of these aspects of ourselves that initiates our journey into becoming fully human, fully incarnated, and more open to love and joy.

This story began as we were growing up. When we formed our identities, we generally identified with characteristics, feelings, ideas, and attitudes that we felt would make our lives work, and these qualities came to represent what we thought were our strengths and best values. In other words, we developed our own unconscious lists of virtues and vices to guide us.

When these identifications begin to fail, people come in to see us professionally, because they have become unhappy or discontent. Or perhaps they were never able to form a workable list or are continually failing to achieve their fantasy of a good life and want their suffering to stop. Two things make it possible for our suffering to begin to stop. First is the acceptance of our suffering—remember self-compassion is needed, not self-judgment. Acceptance is the necessary first step in transforming anything psychological, according to Jung. But our next question is, what will our suffering be transformed into? The answer, according to Jung, is not into peace and joy but into true suffering, which means facing the real early wounds within ourselves and the truth of our inner contradictions. The second thing we must do is value the inhabitants of our shadows—the parts of ourselves that have been disowned, devalued, rejected, and repressed. This all starts with some of our most negative feelings and self-critical voices.

Let me share with you again the *New York Times* article on *The Red Book*:

> Creating the book also led Jung to reformulate how he worked with clients, as evidenced by an entry the editor and translator, Shamdasani, found in a self-published book written by a former client, in which she recalls Jung's advice for processing what went on in the deeper and sometimes frightening parts of her mind.

> "I should advise you to put it all down as beautifully as you can—in some beautifully bound book," Jung instructed. "It will seem as if you were making the visions banal—but then you need to do that—then you are freed from the power of them...Then when these things are in some precious book you can go to the book and turn over the pages and for you it will be your church—your cathedral—

the silent places of your spirit where you will find renewal. If anyone tells you that it is morbid or neurotic and you listen to them—then you will lose your soul—for in that book is your soul."

Knowing our shadow is becoming aware of the parts of our personalities that we have repressed or disassociated from in our development and early adjustment, both good and bad.

Questions to Expand Our Understanding

This is a good time to make these thoughts a little more personal. Here are some quotations and related questions to journal about:

1. "Nothing in our shadow frightens us more than our own denied and impoverished potentials." Valuing our negativity? Making it sacred? What do you think of these ideas?

2. "Loving yourself means knowing there are parts you do not like, parts you are afraid of, parts you keep imprisoned. You are a complex person containing all human potentials." What kinds of feelings come up in you when you think about the various aspects and potentials within your personality?

Paths to Knowing Our Shadows

Paths to Knowing Our Shadows

1. Dreams—same-sex people in our dreams
   a. What are your associations with or to these people specifically, or in general if you don't know them?
   b. What are they doing in your dream? How are they behaving? What do you think about their character?
   c. Are you attracted by them or repelled by them?
   d. Are you afraid of them, disgusted by them, and so on?

2. Projections
   a. Note the irrational strength of our feeling about someone.
   b. Note our difficulty in getting rid of these feelings.

There are two primary paths that we can follow in looking for our shadows. The first one is in dreams. Figures who are the same sex as we are represent shadow aspects of ourselves. Let me give you a brief example. A few days ago a man told me a dream. It had followed a long and somewhat controversial discussion he had the previous evening with his wife. In the dream he was at a celebration with former president Clinton. When I asked him what his associations were with President Clinton, he said that Clinton was a completely political animal. He went on to say that he could not tell if Clinton truly had any values or not, because he always seemed to be compromising what he said he believed in, for political expediency. As you can imagine, while he was talking his face began to change its expression as he recognized himself in how he dealt with his wife.

In projections, the second pathway to our shadows, the irrational strength of our feelings and our inability to get rid of them alert us to the idea that this is our issue, no matter how justified we feel otherwise. The resentments that keep us from going to sleep and the arguments that go on and on in our minds illustrate that projections are at work. In an extreme case we may see someone who seems to personify all that is shifty, cowardly, or evasive. That person will arouse in us dislike, animosity, and even fear. We will find it impossible to be fair with him or her.

Such people are unbearable to us because they stand for something within ourselves that we do not wish to own. They also enable us to maintain our good opinion of ourselves because they carry our rejected, bad qualities or, in some cases, good qualities that we might otherwise have to acknowledge as our own.

Getting to know our shadows is a painful journey because we must crucify our own good opinions of ourselves. The mystics aptly termed this process the "purification of the self." Literature and mythology refer to this process as a "descent" that requires faith, courage, and usually a guide.

I think that it is probably apparent at this point that the realization of our shadow will compel us to outgrow our parents' psychology. And it will compel us to become aware of and outgrow our society's psychology. Both of these are closely tied in with our shadow. Parents, our parental homes, police officers, as well as institutions and their representatives often show up in our dreams in order to help us come to grips with conventional attitudes and values we have internalized.

Process of Detachment

The psychological process of viewing our ego development in relation to our families' and society's psychology, values, and needs is akin to the mystical process of detachment, which is part of the process of purification.

The process of detachment has several levels:

1. Poverty: This means giving up the things that chain our spirits. In the parable of the rich young man, it was not the man's wealth but his attachment to it that caused Jesus to admonish him to give it up. Wealth may often symbolize the values of one's traditions, parents, and culture.

2. Chastity: This means to keep the personality (the soul, in religious terms) open only to the inner voice of the Self (the Divine within).

3. Obedience: This means to follow the razor's edge of the inner voice and to become strengthened and refined by the conflicts between that inner voice and conventional values and wisdom.

The next step for the mystics is mortification, which in our language is the final realization of the shadow. Through mortification we bring our old personality into the spirit and form of the new, enlarged one. The interesting point about this kind of work is that it is never over, and it is always enriching. This is true because the more light we create, the more shadow we create. Does that make sense?

Before I conclude my discussion on the realization of the shadow, there are two things I want to say about this work that can be very real at times. The first one is that there will be times when we discover things within ourselves that are so shocking to us that we can only bow our heads in solemn sorrow before the truth of what we are in that regard. And when we can accept these things about ourselves in the full truth of what we are, it is at that point, Dr. Jung tells us, that the true gold of our humanity begins to glow. The second thing I want to share with you is that the only bad emotions we have are the ones we don't want to admit.

Questions for Reflection

1. How are you feeling personally about what we have been discussing?
2. Take time to journal some of your feelings and reflections.

The Story

We have been talking about transformation, the realization of our shadows, and the journey to bring us to wholeness, the journey motivated by our Holy Longing. When we have lost touch with the mythic depths of the stories in our religious traditions, we can also find threads of transformation and spiritual understanding in other stories, such as fairy tales, that have emerged from our collective unconscious. These stories can also point out the path of restoration and healing if we can become open to the power of the story.

The Grimms' fairy tale "The Water of Life" illustrates this point in a striking way. Even the title has a spiritual, transformative overtone. As you read it, I invite you to think of the different characters as possible distinct tendencies in your own psyche; these characters may depict how you think, feel, or act at times, or they may embody someone or something inside of yourself you turn to or would like to turn to for help. Think too about the roles of despair and betrayal in our lives and how when all things once again become new, the distress of the past recedes. So, here is the fairy tale:

The Water of Life

There was once a king who was so ill that no one believed he would survive. He had three sons who were extremely upset about it and who went down into the palace garden and wept. There they met an old man who asked them why they were so sad. They told him about their father, and that nothing seemed to cure him. He replied, "I know of one more remedy, and that is the water of life; if he drinks of it, he will become well again; but it is hard to find."

The eldest son went to the king and begged to be allowed to go for the water which would heal him. The king said, "No, the danger of it is too great. I would rather die." But his son begged until the king consented. The son thought, "If I bring the water, then I shall be best loved of my father, and shall inherit the kingdom." He set out on his horse and soon met a dwarf, who asked, "Whither away so fast?"

The young man said, "Silly shrimp, it is nothing to do with you," and rode on. But the angry dwarf wished him an evil wish, and soon the eldest son rode between two mountains that grew ever closer until he was totally stuck between them. As he did not return, the second son, with the same ambition to inherit, persuaded his father to let him go. He met exactly the same fate as the eldest. So it goes with haughty people.

The youngest son persuaded his father to let him go. When the dwarf questioned his haste, he stopped and said, "I am seeking the water of life, for my father is sick unto death." The dwarf rewarded his good behavior with the information that the water of life was in the courtyard of an enchanted castle; but to enter the iron door he must strike three times with an iron wand, and he must feed two hungry lions with two loaves of bread. Then he must fetch the water and leave the castle by twelve or be imprisoned there.

All went well as the dwarf had said. Within the castle were enchanted princes whose rings he took from their fingers; a sword and a loaf of bread he took with him; and a beautiful maiden who kissed him and said he had set her free and could marry her if he returned in a year, but warned him to get out with the water before twelve. But the prince lay down wearily on a beautifully made bed, fell asleep, and woke at quarter to twelve. In a fright, he fetched a cup of the water of life and barely made it out of the iron door, which cut off a piece of his heel as it clanged shut.

The prince, rejoicing at having the water, met the dwarf again, who told him that the sword he now had could slay whole armies and the bread would never be used up. The young man begged the dwarf to release his brothers from their imprisonment; the dwarf did so with the warning that they had bad hearts. But the youngest son told them all about the water of life and everything else. As they traveled home, he loaned his sword and his bread to the kings of three different kingdoms devastated by war and famine, so that all of them achieved peace and plenty. Then, as the three brothers went over the sea and the youngest slept, the two eldest plotted and stole the water of life from him, putting salt water into his cup instead.

When they got home, the salt water brought by the youngest made the king sicker than ever; upon which the elder brothers gave the king the water of life and he recovered his health.

They warned the youngest son to say nothing, and the king, thinking the latter had plotted to kill him, grew angry, sentenced him to death and ordered a huntsman to take him into the forest and shoot him.

Once in the forest, the huntsman could not carry out the sentence and confessed all to the prince, who was shocked. The prince begged the huntsman to change clothes with him and then went further into the forest while the huntsman returned home. After a time, three wagon-loads of gold and precious stones came to the king, sent by the three kings whose kingdoms had been saved by the sword and the bread of the youngest son. The king began to wonder, "Can my son have been innocent?" and openly admitted his grief that he had had him killed. Then the huntsman told him the truth, and a stone fell from the king's heart. He let it be known that the prince was in favor and might return home.

Meanwhile, the princess had a bright golden road made leading up to her palace, and gave instructions that only one person who rode straight up it would be the right one, and not any one riding alongside it. The year was now nearly up, so the eldest son thought he would go to claim her as her savior, and the kingdom as well. So he rode in haste, but when he saw the road, he thought, "It would be a sin and a shame if I were to ride over that," and went along the right side. At the palace, he was turned away. The second prince set out and, likewise fearing to damage the road, rode on the left side, with the same result. But now, as the year was entirely up, the third son rode out from the forest toward the palace.

He yearned so incessantly for the princess, with whom he could forget his sorrows that he never noticed the golden road at all and rode right up the middle of it. So he was welcomed as her savior and the lord of the kingdom, and they were married. She told him his father had forgiven him, and he went home, and told the king how his brothers had betrayed him and yet he had kept silent. The father wanted to punish them, but they had put to sea, never to return.

Questions to Expand Our Understanding

As you reflect upon the story, let me ask you a few questions about it:

1. Was anything in the story puzzling to you? Did any part of it cause you to feel uncomfortable?
2. Where did you feel energized or engaged?
3. Which character touched you the most?
4. What associations did you make with the story?
5. How did you feel at the end of the story?

Quotes for Reflection

To further the exploration of our Holy Longing, I've gathered some quotes for you to read and reflect upon. Take five or ten minutes to write your reflections about each of the following statements:

(A) Betrayal, trauma, conflict—these are the fire that can consume the old so that new consciousness can arise like the phoenix and restore our connections to life on a more profound level. In this process we must face the questions: Who am I? Why am I here? Is there a reality I can trust? Is there love I can trust? At these times we are faced with four choices:
  1. Denial—we can throw ourselves into the collective stream of busyness.
  2. Despair and depression, which are often caused by denial and repression.
  3. Regressive restoration of the persona—let's just keep everything looking good and positive.
  4. Step into the flames so that we can arise with transformed consciousness and the renewed personality of the phoenix.

(B) Awakening the Holy, the longing for wholeness, means acknowledging the desires of our hearts to fill our lives with love and transformation, which may not be for something new but for a new way of appreciating who we are, what we have and finding the way to accept our lives as good. In other words, we may be transforming the way we see ourselves and life. Awakening and transforming are

88

often finding new lenses for our perceptions, clearing away the lens clouded by our wounds, complexes, and indoctrinations. Then our lives can be filled with the power of the soul.

(C) Our ego must become small and a servant-leader to the Self, which means it must also become very strong. It gains strength as it is tempered in the fires of transformation, becoming able to roar and be even more ferocious than ever, while at the same time becoming small, realizing its duty as a servant-leader to the Self, earthly and humble not through the realization of the shadow, but through the continuing realization of the shadow. This happens as we learn that a life being fully lived into the Holy Longing is a life of continuing transformation.

(D) This journey requires a deep awakening, a profound change of perspective that makes our tempering sacred. It is a perspective that helps us understand the journey is glorious and leads to a kind of fulfillment beyond what we could imagine. If we keep the old conventional point of view that we are failing, dysfunctional, or have problems, we frequently will feel beat down and defeated with self-criticism and discouragement. The key to the pursuit of our Holy Longing is the awakening.

(E) Hope requires trust and relates to the future. Anxiety also relates to the future, which can fill us with anxiety or hope. But hope that is not a fantasy or naïve must be grounded in "religio"—that is, it must be grounded in the kind of trust that comes from our being related to the source of our being. This kind of hope pulls us into the future, brings a sense of safety, and is an unseen vision that supports our taking risks.

(F) There is a way to have a miraculous life and that is by
1. having the courage to face our negative and dark aspects.
2. having the courage to question all of our experiences.
3. having the courage to profoundly value life, both inner and outer.
4. having the courage to never give up the quest for meaning.

5. accepting that we must be willing to be constantly transformed.
6. realizing that being transformed means giving up an old life or state of mind completely and starting all over again.
7. being wise enough to know we must always start at the bottom, with the rejected, the ugly, and the distasteful.
8. being wise enough to know that seeking love, peace, and happiness always leads to illusion and that if we have the courage to go from the bottom up, all of these things will eventually find us.

Questions to Expand Our Understanding

There are two questions I would like to ask you:

1. What surprised you about this experience?
2. What moved or inspired you the most?

Things I Have Learned on My Own Journey
from my book *The Fire and the Rose*

Four truths have become apparent to me in my own pursuit of self-knowledge as a way of life:

First, I have learned that the fundamental assertion in most mystical traditions—that self-knowledge is the way to come to know the Divine—is absolutely true. Self-knowledge releases us from the prison of our personal history, de-conditions us from the attitudes of our parents and society, and forces us to work through our losses, hurts and grief. This act of purification, as the mystics call it, opens us to our depths, to the Self, the Divine energy within us.

90

The **second** truth I realized is that compassion must begin with myself. The cultivation of compassion toward my failures, short-comings, and humanness opens the door to self-love and makes me a truly compassionate person with others. This process grounds us in our full humanity, and supports the self-love implied in the command-ment, "Love your neighbor, as yourself." Self-love anchored in self-knowledge is the underpinning of how well we can give and receive love. Without self-love, our structure of relationships will crumble un-der the pressure of the smallest storms, and our so-called unselfish acts will create an inner cauldron of resentment. I know this from the results of many years when I thought I could be hard on myself, and loving to others. The only person I fooled was myself. Self-love is like water flowing into a pond. When the pond is full, the water will over-flow and begin to venture into the world. If we fail to know and love ourselves, we risk causing our souls to become arid and our hearts to stagnate in fear and defensiveness. What a wonderful paradox—loving ourselves is actually taking care of others.

The **third** thing I discovered is that a life based on the pursuit of self-knowledge continually takes us back into the world and among our communities. Living a whole-hearted life cannot be done alone. We must participate in all the various relationships—attractions, love, friendships, conflicts, projections—to gain stimulation as well as the content that informs much of our search for self-knowledge.

The final thing that I gradually became aware of is that something inside of me cares about me and my life. If I listen, it speaks to me through my dreams, fantasies, inspiration, and thoughts. When I reflect, journal, and work with my active imagination, it helps heal my wounds, turns my symptoms and failures into lessons, and aids me in discerning what my soul wants for my life. It does not save me from any of life's difficulties or catastrophes. But when I am suffer-ing, it is there with me.

I have called this something the Self over the course of this book. As an analyst, I have studied and worked with the concept of the Self for many years. I have seen the validity of this concept by not-ing how it works in my life and in the lives of the people I counsel professionally. Today I experience the Self very personally, instead of viewing it from the distance of psychological theory. While I am not a theologian, I believe my interactions with the Self are a true experience of feeling the love of the Divine.

PART THREE

BECOMING WHOLE AS A SPIRITUAL NECESSITY: A Jungian Guide for Renewing the Mystic Vision

---

"Mysticism, then, is seen as the 'one way out' for the awakened spirit of man; healing that human incompleteness which is the origin of our divine unrest... To sum up, Mysticism is seen to be a highly specialized form of that search for reality, for heightened and completed life, which we have found to be a constant characteristic of human consciousness."

— EVELYN UNDERHILL, *MYSTICISM*, P. 93

"... 'Only the Real can know Reality.' Awakening, Discipline, Enlightenment, Self-surrender, and Union are the essential phases of life's response to this fundamental fact; the conditions of our attaining of Being... We are, then, one and all the kindred of the mystics."

— EVELYN UNDERHILL, *MYSTICISM*, P. 446

Chapter 5 : Lecture

BECOMING WHOLE
AS A SPIRITUAL NECESSITY: A Jungian
Guide for Renewing the Mystic Vision

The Loss of Soul in Our Religious World

I would like to begin with a few comments on my own experience of the loss of soul in our religions. Whenever I begin to think about religion or spirituality, my memory takes me back to my childhood years when my mother was dying of cancer. Slowly over the period leading up to her death, when I was fourteen, my grief turned into anger, and I found no comfort in the church I had been growing up in. My childhood image of God was incinerated in what I felt was the bleak unfairness of that situation. Entering adolescence, I was left without a religious or spiritual structure that could give me faith in life or a vision of the future that offered purpose and a promise of fulfillment.

The larger trend that my experience brings to mind is the way religion and spirituality have changed since my mother died in 1951. My early trauma thrust me into the front line of changing religious history. As I lived into these times, I stayed stuck in my anger with God for several decades, until I realized that I had one of two choices: regress into fundamentalism or begin a search. Being an agnostic or an atheist or simply believing in a generic higher power doesn't work when you are mad at God. Eventually, I began to realize that life is dynamic and spirituality, like consciousness, must be continually developed or it will fail.

When I was small, my mother took me to a Protestant church where, unfortunately, I learned that I could never be good enough and that loving your neighbor meant always forgiving and helping everyone else or, in reality, pleasing everybody else and never letting yourself be vulnerable to criticism. Plus there was this strange image of God, who could simultaneously love me unconditionally and send me to burn in hell if I wasn't good. Regrettably, the teachings of my childhood contained no hint that love can be the foundation of our being or that life can be a spiritual journey with purpose and meaning or—which would have been even more surprising—that I could find renewal and growth through my personal conflicts and suffering.

The fact is that our religious institutions have been slipping into what we might call the neurosis of the modern age for at least the better part of the last two centuries. In Jungian terms, *neurosis* means "to become increasingly one-sided, unbalanced, and cut off from one's depths." Neurosis is accompanied by a corresponding loss of meaning that brings on fear, anxiety, and regressions into the past. As the neurotic cycle between fear and defensiveness develops, the situation becomes worse.

We know all too well that many of us have had disappointing, disillusioning, and even damaging experiences in our religious institutions. And as a result of these experiences, we see the sexism, hypocrisy, literalism, power drives, sexual obsessions, and exclusivity in these establishments. But rather than simply throwing up our hands, we can turn to our psychological perspective, which will help us recognize that these are symptoms of the old authoritative, and easily understandable, religious ways breaking down, losing their significance, and calling for transformation.

But more than this is going on here. Many of us feel betrayed as I did, and in fact we are. Jung points out in his "Commentary on *The Secret of the Golden Flower*" that all of the great religions are meant to be therapies for the soul as it travels the difficult path of life. When they fail at this task, we feel betrayed—often angry and alienated—because we have lost our support for the soul on its journey through life. To make matters even more difficult, we ourselves are actually being called upon to treat the neuroses of our religious organizations and the pain they are inflicting upon us and our culture.

What this all means is that as our institutions flounder and regress spiritually or grow in darker directions, we, as individuals, are being called upon to carry the responsibility for our own spiritual lives—a responsibility our ancestors projected onto the church or temple, as many people still do or try to do. Other people simply go into denial or look for a new religion to project this responsibility onto.

The reality is that as we grow in consciousness and complexity, institutions can no longer carry this responsibility for us. From the Jungian standpoint, spirituality is an instinct and there is a religious function in our psyche. Denial or repression of this reality leads us to serve the idols of our neurosis or our culture or to fill these needs with addictions. This perspective doesn't mean that our institutions are no longer important or that they should be closed down. It means the responsibility for our spiritual lives is ours to face, and the mystics can show us a way to do this.

As my own journey of discovery continued and after being furious with God for a few decades, I found myself in Zurich in analysis with Dr. John Mattern. (I was in Zurich training to become a Jungian analyst.) John quietly told me that anyone who was as mad with God as I was must be in for a lifelong spiritual quest. This perspective in my analysis at the time and my upcoming exam in religion led me to explore spirituality in a way I had never considered before. I began this new journey by writing a paper comparing Jung's individuation process, the psychological journey into wholeness, with the path of mystical development.

During my research, I discovered that in the past, and in most of the great religions, there was a special group of people who did know how to undertake a journey that led to experiencing the love of the Divine, to loving the Divine, and to having their lives enlarged through these experiences. These people understood the paradox that like lovers, in order to find themselves they must be willing to lose themselves. To lose yourself in this way, you must first become fully yourself, which means becoming a person unique and independent from the effects of your early wounds, scripts, and indoctrinations that have structured your identity.

Pursuit of Self-Knowledge

In the parallel between mystical development and individuation, we find that the Divine or the Self (and that is *Self* with a capital *S*, meaning the center and ground of our being) is found within us through the pursuit of self-knowledge. Once found and related to, the Self becomes a recognized force that wants to shape, form, and inspire our lives and push us to become someone beyond who we could have planned, educated, or imagined ourselves to be.

So, Jungian psychology broke the barriers set up by my early religious experiences and led me into an understanding of spirituality. Jung taught me that the quest for spiritual and psychological maturity is founded upon the quest for self-knowledge and always has been. Jung's concept of individuation was profoundly informed by the works of the mystics and Jung's personal struggle with his own evolving vision or image of God.

The pursuit of self-knowledge, which our culture has trouble valuing, carries us through the four stages of individuation. Individuation is a long journey into personal consciousness that begins as we free ourselves from the dominance of attitudes and behaviors learned from our families and culture as well as what we think we learned from our earlier failures and successes and all of their supporting levels of illusion. On this path, the actions of our lives become increasingly authentic, and they begin disclosing our unique potentials to others in an expression that contributes to life.

This line of thinking brings to mind Evelyn Underhill, the great Anglican scholar of mysticism. She describes the mystical path in a similar way and calls it the development of spiritual consciousness. Like individuation, it is a process of growth, of continuing transformation. Here is a list of Underhill's eight stages for this process. All of these stages are based on self-examination and a belief that development is fueled by increasing self-knowledge and an unfolding of awareness of the Divine presence operating in one's life.

Terms

reality, lowercase *r*—the symbol of our busy, everyday reality; in psychological terms, the reality of the ego—the world of Jung's number one personality

Reality, uppercase *R*—the symbol of Eternal Reality, from which the mystery and life force pours into our world and experience; the world of the collective unconscious and the Self; The Self may be seen as the divine spark, which the mystics see in each of us, that gives us our life force and the feeling of life's mystery and that contains the unique pattern and potential for our lives. Jung connected his number two personality to this world.

The Green Lion

symbolizes the self-responsible adult that is still spiritually undeveloped but has the strength and vitality to live successfully on the material, everyday level; a person who has developed an identity, a certain amount of ego strength, ego ideals, a workable persona, and who functions responsibly in society

The Red Dragon

symbolizes the transformed Green Lion that has gone through the mystical process of growth and transformation and lives with equal power on the material and spiritual planes; a person who has progressed far enough in his or her development of consciousness to realize the ego must be transformed from a position of "I want" to "I serve"—that is, "I serve" the Self or Divine within; This entails growth into the fourth stage of consciousness as outlined in *Sacred Selfishness* and the journey that includes. The Red Dragon is a person of substance who glows with the love of life and creates a force field that encourages others to glow.

Why Is Awakening So Important?

Later in this lecture, I am going to reduce these eight stages to four—awakening, the purgative way, the illuminative way, and the unitive way—which to some extent sum up all eight. Each stage presents us with a new task and offers the promise of a further transformed life.

Now, why is there such concern for stage one: awakening, or becoming psychologically and spiritually conscious? Our mythology and wisdom traditions answer this question. Throughout the world our creation stories begin with light because light is a metaphor for

Eight Stages of Mystical Growth Chart

from Evelyn Underhill's *Mysticism: The Nature and Development
of Spiritual Consciousness*

1. **AWAKENING** In this stage, you become aware in some way that the world isn't what you thought it was and you are not who you thought you were. There is a disturbance of personal equilibrium that brings an awareness of a larger world, no longer under control, and that leaves one feeling small, like a child. There is the beginning of the twofold nature of the Divine—it is both being and becoming. Because of our society's distance from spiritual understanding, our calls to awaken often come as personal crises, emotional and physical symptoms, mistakes, and difficulties that threaten our equilibrium and feelings of safety and direction. Thus we are called to seek help.

2. **PURIFICATION** This stage requires practices that help one reclaim a relationship with the interior life. It also demands commitment and intentional activity with the goal of ridding oneself of the veils and illusions of the unexamined life. Spiritual practices focus on a release from the old ways and illusions. This stage calls for heroic passions in the soul. Psychology or analysis can be a similar process of self-examination and seeking self-knowledge that will continue through all of the stages. During purification, one seeks to identify wounds, attitudes and other influences that have driven one's life, creating the illusions of our perceptions and the ideas of who we are.

3. **ILLUMINATION** In this stage, one begins to see the beauty and patterns in life. Life intensifies; perception is exalted; feelings of suffering, joy, and love become clear experience. Intuition and an appreciation for the transcendent aspects of life grow. One lives in two worlds, with vocation in ordinary reality but with a steady relationship with the Divine. Psychologically, we continue the journey into individual consciousness and the pursuit of self-knowledge. Emphasis is on getting to know the shadow— the various parts of oneself and how to relate to them and apprehend a pattern in one's life while also becoming grounded in one's humanity. Practices such as befriending dreams, journaling, and active imagination become increasingly important.

4. **VOICES AND VISIONS** In this stage, one sees, hears, and interacts with a larger Reality. This includes dreams and visions for the mystic. One sees and hears with more than the five senses, and this is a state of revealing and interacting with a much larger Reality. Psychologically, dream work and active imagination become more important. Archetypal patterns—particularly shadow, anima, animus—are revealed. Intuition intensifies. One is well into the stage of individual consciousness and is aware of the Self and its energy.

5. **INTROVERSION** Quietness, silence, and prayer become the mainstay of the mystical life and a refuge and a place of renewal from the busy world of ordinary reality. Quietness opens one to the journey to the center and requires a new refusal of the values of ordinary reality. There is a renewed openness to rapture and joy as one finds the resources of the center. Psychologically, inner work is seen as pleasure, renewal, and the ground of one's continued growth. It brings contentment as well as relief, comfort, and direction when times are troubling. Inner work also brings the assurance we are part of something bigger that supports us—that is, the ego is supported by the unconscious and the Self.

6. **ECSTASY AND RAPTURE** For the mystics this stage is about the art and science of happiness, the openness to love, a feeling of union with the Divine and the knowledge that spiritual storms enhance vitality. In the past this stage was often experienced physically as a trance state. Emotionally, it is a feeling of unity and enhanced perception. Psychologically, one has reached the point in individual consciousness where one feels at home in oneself and life. Self-knowledge is bringing balance to living. Love and other relationships no longer reflect illusions, needy psychological pursuits, or idealistic fantasies. Nor does one's self-image reflect illusions. One has learned self-forgiveness and self-love as a foundation for loving others and life.

7. **DARK NIGHT OF THE SOUL** This stage is the time of further destruction and construction of one's interior. It is the mystic death of an old state of consciousness and the birth of a new one. It requires surrender, and suffering tests one's love when God seems to have disappeared and everything goes wrong. Psychologically, this is a time when we realize that growth and individuation aren't what we thought they were. Joy disappears. One faces the remaining specters of old forms, habits, attitudes, and emotional problems again, as further preparation for growth. The ego is being put through the stage of transformation from "I want" to "I serve" the Self or the Divine within.

8. **THE UNITIVE LIFE** For the mystic, there is a unification of the personality on a higher level. Knowledge, will, and love are joined and satisfied and serve the Divine. Life is filled with a transcendent vitality and heroic activity. Being and becoming are joined. There is a marriage of the soul and the Divine. Psychologically, this stage is reflected in the state of illuminated consciousness, which is the realization of one's unique personality and its relationship to one's deeper Self and all life. The ego is able to live in relationship and service to the Self. The search for self-knowledge is a natural choice in life, as is growth. The person has become a person of "substance" who loves life and gives energy, vitality, and hope to the people around him or her.

human consciousness rising from the dark waters of the unconscious and fostering the origins of life. Throughout all cultures, light means awareness and knowing.

To see the light personally, to begin the creation of our authentic lives, we must awaken. When asked if he was enlightened, the Buddha replied, "No, I am awake." The Sanskrit roots of the word *Buddha* mean "one who has awakened." The word is related to the Sanskrit words meaning "understanding" and "intelligence." A person who has awakened can therefore be said to be "one who knows"—one who has awakened to the true nature of reality. Two of Christ's miracles address this same point metaphorically when he makes the blind see and the deaf hear. And a major purpose in Jungian analysis is to bring healing, wholeness, and meaning into our lives by discovering the truth—being able to see the truth—of our own reality.

The importance of awakening is dramatically emphasized by the twentieth century theologian Reinhold Niebuhr when he says, "Most evil is not done by evil people, but by good people who don't know what they are doing." This sentence is too important not to repeat—"Most evil is not done by evil people, but by good people who don't know what they are doing." I am going to continue to emphasize awakening, because it took me many frustrating years and experiences to realize that awakening is not a one-time event. Growth and transformation are meant to be continuous cycles, and each cycle begins with a new awakening.

The mystics consider us all to be asleep or caught in the trance of conventional life and the way we were taught to adapt to it. While we are in this trance, we share the thoughts that we know who we really are, that we are able to make conscious choices, and that we understand the complexities of the issues facing us. In the unconsciousness of this position, we continue to choose our destructive ways and blame other people and outer events for our frustrations. We do this because we fail to realize that we are looking at life through the lens of our adaptive identity and our personal and cultural complexes.

Awakening from this trance—truly seeing and hearing—means developing consciousness through self-knowledge. C. S. Lewis amplifies this point in his sermon "The Weight of Glory" when he says we desire too little out of life and fail to imagine the spiritual rewards available to us. Carl Jung asserts that this whole affair is about more than personal fulfillment when he points out that the fate of the world hangs by the slender thread of human consciousness. And if we stop and think for a minute, we can see how frightfully true these two statements are.

So, the first question that may come to mind is, how do we begin awakening and proceed to becoming spiritually conscious? The reality is that we must continue to pursue self-awareness in order to know when we are being called to awaken. And we must learn from our experiences of awakening and growth that what we seek is hidden within ourselves.

The word *mystic* derives from the Greek word *myein*, which means "closing the eyes or the lips," and the word *mystikos*, meaning "one who has been initiated." Together these meanings explain that we must distance ourselves from everyday life, protect this process, and go through a procedure leading to initiated knowledge. Therefore the mystical path is structured to help us develop self-knowledge in a manner that is constantly transforming and initiates us into new levels of consciousness. This process results in a more complete experience of being alive and a more personal relationship with the Divine.

As we pursue this kind of knowledge, we discover that spiritual growth is not a matter of faith based on blind belief. Nor is it an intellectual faith that consists of giving assent to creeds and doctrines. Spiritual growth is committing ourselves to the inner way, regardless of what comes, a determination to know the One who is at the center of our being. Commitment, devotion, dedication reflect the mystic giving his or her heart to the process of mystical growth.

The resulting faith, which is more akin to trust than belief, is then more personal and based on the inner experience. Built of essential spiritual material that is difficult to threaten, this kind of faith is well rooted in personal and sacred substance and, therefore, responds to threats with laughter and compassion and not with anger and aggression.

Not too long ago I had an experience that opened my eyes. In the middle of the night, I was reading the letters between Dr. Jung and Victor White—the Dominican monk, Jungian analyst, and theology

103

professor. For most of my life, I've liked to read in bed until I slowly go to sleep. On this particular evening, I'd been reading for about an hour. Jung and White were carrying on about the *privatio boni* and I was getting bored and sleepy.

Then all of a sudden: Wham! I was sitting straight up in bed. In his letter of April 3, 1954, White is confessing his loss of faith and his fear of needing to leave the church. And Jung, 80 years old, is answering as the great doctor of the soul, and it left me so charged up I couldn't sleep for hours. Jung says to Father White that even the church is alive only to the extent that it is able to change, to give old truths new forms, and to carry forward the meanings of these truths, rather than just their words. Jung emphasizes that if you try to be literal about doctrine, you deaden your religious experience and remain asleep. Rather than swallowing doctrine whole, he suggests we struggle with it, disagree with it—even if we recognize its importance for the majority. In this process, doctrine transforms us and we transform it. Moreover, if we don't struggle and disagree, we have no foundation for helping people who need our understanding as they suffer from these same difficulties.

I shudder when I think of how many years I've spent beating my head against the wall of needing to either swallow or deny doctrine without looking at the issue in a more profound way. Jung went on to advise White to be true to his mythos, its meaning, and his vocation and to quit worrying about who believed what.

Questions to Expand Our Understanding

1. As I have talked about the neurosis of religion in modern times and the need for self-knowledge and awakening, what kinds of thoughts, memories, and questions came to mind for you?

2. How do you understand the term initiated knowledge, for example, in comparison to what we think of as academic knowledge?

3. What did you think of Reinhold Niebuhr's statement, "Most evil is not done by evil people, but by good people who don't know what they are doing?" Consider, for example, Greek myths in which a lack of conscious awareness invites a tragic fate.

4. What are some of our defenses against our calls to awaken? Think about obligations, responsibilities, good behavior, and so on.

The Anatomy of Healing and Transformation in Individuation and Mysticism

Jung was considered by many as a mystic himself, not only for his knowledge but also for his deep understanding of religion and the human soul. In his last great book, *Mysterium Coniunctionis*, he points out that it is the mystic vision that takes us out of religious decay. The mystics carry the soul force of religion––the love and deep relationship with the Divine. They bear the mystery that can return creativity to religion and transform it into a spiritual quest. The mystic vision arises out of the great religions and becomes critical of their institutions when their dogma has rigidified. The mystics replace fear with awe, authority with compassion, and duty with love. They reclaim the true purpose of dogma—which is to channel our relationship to the numinous and to support and liberate spiritual growth, not limit it. Like that of the mystics, much of Carl Jung's mission in life was to free religion and spiritual consciousness from their self-imposed shackles.

Mysticism breaks the mold of our approach to religion and returns us to the ground or source of our being and to our capacity to experience and relate to the Divine—which means to life—from our hearts. And, once again, this is the daily work that many of us, as analysts, do with our analysands, hour by hour.

Under the attack of the modern era's obsession with rational thinking, the Western religions' soul-arousing symbols—their mythic language and rituals, in other words, their mythos—have been lost or devalued. Even though some of these symbols still affect people, those worshippers rarely understand why they do, and therefore rarely experience true transformation.

The Way to Wholeness

Jung beautifully explains how the Divine influenced his own life in his autobiography, *Memories, Dreams, Reflections*; he says, "I find that all of my thoughts circle around God like the planets around the sun, and are as irresistibly attracted by him." This comment in his late years led me to understand his writings in a new way, as well as why the most important of his works deal with the religious problems of Christianity.

He looked at religious problems from the standpoint of psychology, which means he stressed understanding and reflection, rather than belief. Jung explained the transforming mysteries of the Mass with such moving thoroughness that his work inspired me to return to religion. In my experience, Jungian psychology takes in and integrates religion in a way that neither reduces nor damages its value. Instead, the spiritual is confirmed, amplified, and made more understandable as an active part of life.

Like the mystics, Jung thought that the Divine must be known through personal experience and that secondhand belief systems never adequately fill our spiritual longings. Yet he also said that such systems could be a very good defense against true experiences of the Divine *and the resulting need to change our lives*—which such an experience always brings.

The mystics see the mystical journey as the way of salvation. The root meaning of *salvation* is "the way of redemption" or "the way to wholeness." What the mystics mean here is that their path bridges our everyday reality and Eternal Reality. These two realities become equal parts of the unitive way as Eternal Reality informs everyday reality and one enters into a relationship with the Divine. In Jungian psychology, this is the stage in which the ego, our everyday personality, enters into an ongoing relationship to the Self: the center of our being and carrier of the Divine spark within us.

According to the mystics, the nature of the Divine has three characteristics that have parallels in Jungian psychology. The first characteristic is that the Divine nature and the nature of the Self are always *creative* and are expressed as "the spirit of becoming". All true development in human life is based on this creative force. The Jungian analyst and scholar Erich Neumann notes that only Western humanity, in the rigidity of its ego and in its imprisonment in rationality, fails to recognize our dependence on the force that mystically changes us, the force by which we live and that lives within us as our creative center or Self. Our recognition of the Self—the Divine within and our experience of it—becomes the basis for our capacity to transform fate, the hand existence has dealt us, into a fulfilled destiny.

Life is struggle & conflict

A second characteristic of the Divine requires that the spiritually mature person, leading a creative life, develop a *new* version of his or her idea of peace and well-being. The creativity of the Divine always grows out of conflicts, betrayal, tension, and destruction. In the archetypal pattern of growth and transformation—that of life, death, and rebirth—our personality experiences the death aspect as tension, conflict, and destruction. The tension is between our deep values and conventional values or obligations; the conflict is within ourselves and with others over these tensions; and the destruction is of our fantasies and ideas of how things should be or what we want.

We cannot avoid the fact that we must be willing to dissolve our old personalities, our conventional selves—the identities we formed unconsciously for the most part—in the search for the Divine. Paradoxically, the journey that leads to this act or experience simultaneously brings us to the realization of our true Selves. Here we are encountering one of the great truths in mysticism: Dissolution is also creation. The path of transformation is life, death, rebirth—and creation comes from the conflict and destruction taking place in a strongly lived life.

Many years ago, when I was changing careers from business to psychology, I had a dream that illustrated the conflict I was experiencing. I wanted to pursue a new life; in fact I believed that my life depended on this pursuit, which required me to go back to graduate school. Yet I also had children. I greatly valued them and the quality of their lives, which meant I still had to earn a living. In the midst of this conflict, I dreamed I was on a cross. Below me, on my right, was a group of older people, representing traditional values, looking up at me. On my left was a group of children, representing the future, also looking up at me. For the children's sake, I—that is my ego, my sense of identity—was going to have to die and be reborn with a perspective that was broad enough and a heart that was big enough to hold the tensions of this conflict and carry it into the future. Spiritual peace, the peace brought on by the wisdom in the individuation process, is the acceptance of tension and conflict as signs of the Divine presence or the Self at work. The nature of the Divine is creative and it is creativity that overcomes death. True peace comes from accepting this reality.

Now we come to the third characteristic of the mystic vision, which is to encounter the Divine as a lover. This theme permeates the mystical traditions, whether in the poetry of Rumi, the Song of Songs, or Giovanni Bernini's great statue expressing the ecstasy of Divine love experienced by Saint Teresa. But this love is not the love we conventionally think of as love. It is not the shallow version of "Love your neighbor" that was taught in my childhood church. To understand it, one must have walked up the spiral staircase of the development of consciousness beyond childhood wounds and self-alienation and come to the point of understanding that this love is the ground of our very being. In this state, I experience the interconnectedness of all life—not life as an abstraction, but life as it is being lived through me and through you in this moment.

The need for love and relationship is hardwired into our psyche in the same way that makes our need for spirituality an instinct. "Love makes us who we are, and who we can become." This is not the statement of a mystic. This is the statement of three modern psychiatrists devoted to brain research. Mystics believe the need for love is part of the Divine pattern. Science now shows it is part of human nature.

To summarize my last three major points, I want to say that the Divine or the Self is always creative in the sense of the spirit of becoming. The archetypal pattern is that creation grows out of conflicts, tension, betrayal, and destruction, and true peace comes from accepting this fact. And there is an underlying force, which I call love, that is trying to bring us into harmony with life and a passionate experience of life. These three points alone are a lot to awaken to.

In addition, Dr. Jung tells us that being on the journey is the goal. There was a time, before I was truly on the journey, when my goal was to find peace, to transcend my life, or to escape the tension and travail in it. I tried a number of things like Zen meditation, Taoism, therapy, yoga, and so on. They didn't work because I was longing to escape my life, not to confront it and learn the lessons it was trying to teach me. It is very tempting for us to fall into a complete misunderstanding of the spiritual or mystical quest and to see it as a way of escaping the harshness and chaos of living in the world. If we fall into this trap, mysticism becomes a longing for a "paradisical wholeness"—a transcendence of life that I call narcissistic mysticism. In psychological terms, narcissistic mysticism is a rejection of the conflicts, suffering, and imperfections of the world. It wants to dissolve the ego as the bearer of suffering and tension in order to regress into the psychological state of magical unity that is experienced prenatally. In Jungian psychology, the archetypal hero's or heroine's very first task in approaching life is to defeat this longing. Unfortunately, many people think that mystics reject the world in order to transcend it, but in fact the mystic path is to embrace the world in order to sanctify it.

The creative spirit of the Divine shapes life as a journey of personal transformation. Awakening leads to a disciplined process that will strengthen and transform our ego. The ego's purification, struggle, and strengthening create a divinely fortified personality. This transformation is necessary because the soul force of the spirit brings to us power, challenge, and the return of love and longing for the Divine. To the normal ego, which longs for safety, the soul force seems to carry a power of creation that is as demonic as it is Divine, because it destroys and replaces our visions of life. And only the rewards of growth, for ourselves and the culture, justify the pain of this process. to let go & suffer the pain

When transformed, we understand the Divine nature of suffering, conflict, and tension, and we understand that this is how we and the world are differentiated and grow. True peace comes from the acceptance of this dynamism. The creative nature of the Divine is world-forming and world-generating and therefore affirms the world. The mystic path does not lead to dissolution of the ego or of consciousness but to the attainment of transformed consciousness, the center of which has shifted from the ego to the Divine center or Self. Now, let me be careful to point out that ecstatic mysticism and contemplative withdrawal from the world at this point are not the rejection of the world (as they might appear). Such a withdrawal represents an extreme exertion of the ego to transcend the limits of the old personality and to reenergize and strengthen oneself for continual world-transforming activity.

Here is another very important point: As our personal transformation goes on, we begin to help transform the world. What this means is that we live from a deeper sense of purpose and destiny. For the mystic, transformation leads to vocation and mission. In joining the Divine in re-creating and renewing the world, the mystic is called into life, into teaching, writing, establishing schools, and helping to make life a sacred journey—and making life a sacred journey is a call to the mystic in each one of us.

Then as one approaches the knowledge of wholeness, the life-giving effect of the mystical experience becomes vital in what I call ultimate or love mysticism. The reality of the Self or Divine becomes transparent as life is lived and the world is perceived symbolically. Everything in the world becomes a symbol and part of the numinous and is pregnant with the Divine presence. The purpose then is not to plunge into the white primal light and lose our identity but to discover the radiance in all aspects of the world.

For the mystic in this phase, the world is both within and without. In the fullness of life, he or she needs no heaven, no hereafter, no messianic kingdom, for all of this is present in the world, though veiled and hidden. Now the mystic and the Divine meet each other in the open. The world takes form around a united personality, the numinous becomes transparent, and "the fixed star, the star of eternal love," shines through, as Dante reminds us.

Now, so far we have seen that the way of mysticism is very close to that of individuation. In following either path, we have to be willing to awaken to the idea that within us is a true hunger or thirst that isn't being filled. This awakening isn't easy in our culture because we have been strongly indoctrinated to think that if something doesn't seem right or if our life isn't working according to the conventional values, then we're doing something wrong. Questioning ourselves can be frightening. In fact, when our life isn't working in some way—ways that can range from a general feeling of restlessness to addictions, affairs, heart disease, depression, and so on—we need to ask ourselves much bigger questions than whether what we are doing is right or wrong. If we are asking only the right-or-wrong questions, what we are really doing is sublimating and denying our psychological and spiritual needs.

It takes an amazing amount of strength to shift our perspective away from the idea that we are doing something wrong when we have symptoms and difficulties in living, and it takes even more strength to begin to think of these things as potential teachers. In other words, it takes a great deal of strength to shift our perspective to see that the "something" that we think is wrong is trying to get us to change in ways that will help our lives be better on a more profound level. Jung calls this the teleological aspects of symptoms. They are waking us up to the need to learn how to see reality in a new way.

If we accept this perspective, we can see that behind our emotional problems, dissatisfactions, and even physical illnesses are hidden the powerful psychological and spiritual influences that underlie our attitudes toward life and its guiding principles.

Questions to Expand Our Understanding

1. Did anything in this section surprise you or move you?
2. Do you remember the three characteristics related to the Divine or Self?
   a. The Divine is always creative in the sense of "the spirit of becoming."
   b. The Divine requires that the spiritually mature person develop a new version of his or her idea of peace. (We grow through conflicts, sin, mistakes, and failures.)
   c. The Divine can be encountered as a lover. Could you yourself say this about the Self? *Termagami*
3. What do you think about mysticism and individuation as means to developing a full engagement in life?

The Creative Connection: Transmitting the Power of Rebirth

Journey of Purification—Meeting Our Shadow

At this point, it naturally follows to look beyond awakening (which is the first stage in mystical development) to our second stage in mystical development: the purgative way or what we Jungians call the realization of our shadow. These two stages begin to loosen us from the influences in our past. After awakening, the mystics set out on the purgative way. The purgative way, as the name suggests, involves a very committed and

Four Orders of Mysticism Chart

I. **Narcissistic Mysticism** This type of approach represents the longing for a "paradisical wholeness." In psychological terms, narcissistic mysticism is a rejection of the conflicts, suffering, and imperfections of the world. It wants to dissolve the ego as the bearer of suffering and tension in order to regress into the psychological state of magical unity experienced prenatally. This longing for perfection and peace becomes a strong defense against healing and growth and leads into destructive paths of avoidance. In Jungian psychology, the archetypal hero's or heroine's very first task is to defeat this longing. Unfortunately, many people think that mystics reject the world in order to transcend it, but in fact the mystic path is to embrace the world in order to sanctify it.

II. **Transformational Mysticism and the Individual** The individual with a strong ego is awakened and begins the disciplined mystic journey that will strengthen and transform the ego. The ego's purification, struggle, and strengthening create a divinely fortified personality. This transformation is necessary because the soul force of the spirit brings power, challenge, and the return of love and longing for the Divine to us. To the normal ego, which longs for safety, the soul force seems to carry a power of creation that is as demonic as it is Divine, because it destroys and replaces our visions of life. And only the rewards of growth, for ourselves and the culture, justify the pain of this process.

When transformed, we understand the Divine nature of suffering, conflict, and tension, and we understand that this is how we and the world are differentiated and grow. True peace comes from the acceptance of this dynamism. The creative nature of the Divine is world-forming and world-generating and therefore affirms the world. The mystic path does not lead to dissolution of the ego or of consciousness but to the attainment of transformed consciousness, the center of which has shifted from the ego to the Divine center or Self. (Note: Ecstatic mysticism and contemplative withdrawal from the world at this point are not the rejection of the world, as they might appear. Such a withdrawal represents an extreme exertion of the ego to transcend the limits of the old personality and to reenergize and strengthen oneself for continual world-transforming activity.)

III. **Transformational Mysticism and the World** The union of the person or ego with the Divine is possible only if the ego consummates its destiny. Transformation leads to vocation and mission. The intention of the mystic is to join the Divine in the re-creation and the renewal of the world. The duty of self-sacrifice, which has the force of law in all higher mysticism, demands that the mystic teach, write, establish schools, and participate in making life a sacred journey.

112

IV. Ultimate or Love Mysticism As one approaches the knowledge of wholeness, the life-giving effect of the mystical experience becomes vital. The reality of the Self or Divine becomes transparent as life is lived and the world is perceived symbolically. Everything in the world becomes a symbol and part of the numinous and is pregnant with the Divine presence. The purpose, then, is not to plunge into the white primal light and lose our identity but to discover the radiance in all aspects of the world. For the mystic in this phase, the world is both within and without. In the fullness of life, he or she needs no heaven, no hereafter, no messianic kingdom, for all of this is present in the world, though veiled and hidden. Now the mystic and the Divine meet each other in the open. The world takes form around a united personality, the numinous becomes transparent, and the "fixed star, the star of eternal love," shines through.

lengthy process of self-examination. In the mystical tradition, it included examination of conscience, along with the kind of asceticism that would help one detach from worldly values and attachments, particularly the attachment to one's self-image. In the language of the Middle Ages, purgation or purification sums up the process needed to see through our illusions, particularly the ones about who we think we are.

In the work of Jungian psychology, the purgative way is the process of becoming aware of our shadows. Purification parallels our work with our shadows as we explore and bring into consciousness our woundedness, the parts in us—good and bad—that we repressed in order to adapt as we grew up. The work also brings into consciousness the depth of how self-alienated we have become in our journey to adulthood. In this process, we are both healing our experiences of the past and differentiating ourselves from our history, in preparation for reconstructing a bolder, more open, and fully human life that can be more capable of a relationship with the Self or the Divine energy within us.

My struggle to come to grips with religion in my adult life was compounded by the trauma in my earlier life. Because of this trauma, the part of me that is naturally inclined to be religious—the part that is passionate about finding meaning, purpose, and value in my life—had been repressed into my shadow. Confronting my shadow was and is a lot more than confronting bad habits, negative complexes, and my potential for evil. It is also about confronting the depth of my trauma, including the low level of ongoing depression I lived with since that time, and relearning the passionate spiritual devotion to growth and transformation that I am dedicated to.

In my early thirties when I was struggling with decisions about leaving the safety of my life at the time, I had the following dream: A young, golden-haired boy was standing on a hillside in the morning mist. He was motioning for me to join him. Unfortunately, I was too far away to hear what he was calling, but I could see him clearly. Then I noticed I was standing in the hallway of a large, old Victorian-style house. The inside of the house looked the way I imagine an old English men's club would. The walls were paneled in dark wood and the carpets were richly colored. Men in suits and ties were sitting in leather arm-chairs, smoking pipes and cigars while reading newspapers. As I tried to leave the house and join the boy, I felt a powerful force grabbing me around the legs and pulling me back. I woke up struggling for freedom.

The dream was showing me how difficult it is to break away from the traditional values of success and from the rich sense of belonging, to see through the spell of that enchanted domain and seek new life. Along these lines Jung reminds us that in the Christian tradition, we are offered a profound choice as to how to live: Are we going to try to live an imitation of Christ's life, which is difficult enough in itself, or are we going to try to live our own life as true to the Divine pattern within us, as Christ did? The same thing can be said about any of the great religious figures in the major traditions. The mystics and individ-uation make the second choice.

In summary, our first step is to begin to awaken to our need for something more profound in our lives; to awaken to the idea that we are living a life based on illusions; and to awaken to the reality that we are not doing things wrong. We are facing a psychological and spiritual challenge to transform, to grow beyond the security of our present lives, no matter how happy or unhappy they may be. While difficult in its appearance, this moment of spiritual or psychological passage offers great rewards. We do not want to return to normal—we want to grow beyond normal. We may also intuit that pursuing any other course could ultimately be very destructive for us.

At this point I want to repeat that this process does not negate the ego. It is certainly humbling, but being aware of our own broken, wounded places and the potential good and bad that we have denied becomes the beginning of our journey. These places usually hold the guiding spiritual spark that can lead us toward wholeness. The poet Rilke beautifully sums up the paradoxes within our shadows when he says, in a letter to a young poet, "Perhaps all the dragons of our lives are princesses who are only waiting to see us once, beautiful and brave. Perhaps everything terrible is in its deepest being something that needs our love."

The journey of purification or meeting our shadow leads us to a perception of life and reality that is radically different from that of the so-called normal world. Rather than solving or fixing our problems, we are pursuing a spiritual task. Forgiveness, compassion, and loving one's enemies must begin within ourselves. Dr. Jung describes the need for this approach:

> Perhaps this sounds very simple, but simple things are always the most difficult. In actual life, it requires the greatest art to be simple, and so acceptance of oneself is the essence of the moral problem and the acid test of one's whole outlook on life. That I feed the beggar, that I forgive an insult, that I love my enemy in the name of Christ—all these are undoubtedly great virtues. What I do unto the least of my brethren that I do unto Christ. But what if I should discover that the least amongst them all, the poorest of all beggars, the most impudent of all offenders, yea the very fiend himself—that these are within me, and that I myself stand in need of the alms of my own kindness, that I myself am the enemy who must be loved—what then? Then, as a rule, the whole truth of Christianity is reversed: there is then no more talk of love and long-suffering; we say to the brother within us "Raca," [which means "worthless"] and

condemn and rage against ourselves. We hide him from the world, we deny ever having met this least among the lowly in ourselves, and had it been God himself who drew near to us in this despicable form we should have denied him a thousand times before a single cock had crowed.

The Illuminative Way

This process brings us into a new state of consciousness that is referred to by the mystics as the illuminative way. Jung refers to following individuation as fulfilling the Divine pattern within us. He goes on to say, "If I fulfill my pattern, then I can accept my very sinfulness and can say 'It is too bad, but it is so—I have to agree with it.' And then I am fulfilled, then the gold begins to glow." People who can accept and forgive themselves and continue to grow inspire us all. Knowing our shadow, which includes our repressed emotional and instinctual potential for vitality, is the first step in releasing our desire to live a passionate life.

As our perspective transforms, as we go up the spiral staircase of developing consciousness, we understand the necessity of living wholeheartedly. It is our wholehearted engagement with our inner and outer lives that gives us the food for our reflections. Jung underlines that we cannot obtain the knowledge beforehand that can come only as a result of being committed to a full engagement in life. To support his point, he relates the story of Saul's conversion to Paul in the same talk to a clergy convention that I mentioned previously. Jung said, "Saul owed his conversion neither to true love, nor to true faith, nor to any other truth. It was solely his hatred of the Christians that set him on the road to Damascus and to that decisive experience which was to alter the whole course of his life. He was brought to this experience by following out, with conviction, his own worst mistake." In another place, Jung used this story to illustrate that if we pursue the wrong thing with all of our heart, we will end up at the right place.

Now, in the illuminative way we commit to the beauty of life as it is, including our mistakes, without the crippling self-judgment of conventional perspectives. The awareness of ourselves as separate from the forces that molded us invites us into the experience of personal authenticity and of feeling at home within ourselves. The illuminative way challenges us to unite within us a life being lived and our efforts to reflect upon that life. But once we become alert to our need to pay careful attention to our actions, thoughts, feelings, and messages from the unconscious, we discover that this heedfulness is a demanding task.

However, and there is no way around it, spiritual growth throughout history has always been a matter of methodical devotion. If you want a life with meaning, fulfillment, joy, love, and purpose, you have to pay attention to it. These are the fruits of self-knowledge and spiritual development and cannot be obtained any other way. Whatever illusion you distract yourself with—whether it is busyness and obligations or being a pleaser, achiever, or whatever—is simply an excuse for allowing yourself to live a hollow life, an excuse to be, as T. S. Eliot says in "The Hollow Men,"

> Shape without form, shade without colour,
> Paralysed force, gesture without emotion

If, however, we begin to keep a journal, write down our dreams, and do active imagination, several interesting things will happen. We will begin to think in terms of reflecting on our lives or losing them; just the act of "being there" for our soul becomes powerful and life enhancing. The more we examine our lives, the more natural it becomes to see the world in symbolic terms and to realize that the capacity for symbolic vision is the foundation of a conscious and spiritual life. It becomes apparent that if our holy books are not seen through the eyes of metaphor, they lose their ability to inform our lives. And we are led to realize that paying attention is the acid test of love, and we must love ourselves and life in this most important way.

The Unitive Way

And finally, I'll say a few words about the unitive way. As I said earlier, when we examine the root meanings of the word *salvation*, which we hear so often in religious circles, we find that it means "to become intact." Salvation is the way to redemption and the way to wholeness. In individuation and mysticism, the path is the way to wholeness, and the process itself engenders love. As we look at the contribution of Under-hill, we see that the mystics considered the unitive life to be one that reflected a unification of the personality on high levels and that perceived reality with clarity and awareness of its profound implications.

The individuation process—consciously being in life in relationship to our greater Self—leads to a constantly evolving and deepening "I and Thou" relationship with our center. Our greater Self—or the Divine presence within—is an inner companion that teaches, heals, and centers our development. As we realize this presence and learn that it is the One guiding our particular strand into the web of life, the perspective we have on our life story changes dramatically.

Consciousness brings our greatest healing as it links our mind, body, emotions, and spirit into one focused whole. Through consciousness we discover the Self, the Divine within, that infuses our body, mind, and heart with life, love, and creative power and allows us to understand the underlying notion of wholeness that the great religions all suggest.

To feel the sense of wholeness supporting life is like coming home to ourselves. It is a moment of joy and serenity. And although it is a moment we can enjoy, it's not one we can hold on to. If we try, the effort will imprison us in the same way that never wanting to leave home can prevent our journey from continuing. You see, the unitive life is not the top of the spiral staircase. It is a new landing on the staircase. But life as a dynamic force goes on, and we are called to meet new situations, to be creative in new ways, to grow again, to continue the steps toward a new level with another landing.

In this process, we have the opportunity to accumulate the riches of a growing soul—a soul that permeates and enlarges our personality—which becomes an abundant personality in which courage, generosity, compassion, joy, and love come naturally. The goal of this process is to become what the religious writer Frederick Buechner describes as a life-giver: one whose presence breathes life into those whose lives he or she touches. Our choice is whether to allow our souls to congeal into a repetition of what we have done or suffered before or instead to answer the calls from the depths within us that urge us to become life-givers as long as we are alive.

118

Questions to Expand Our Understanding

1. Did anything surprise you in this section?

2. What do you think and feel about Jung's question about self-compassion: "If I should discover...that I myself am the enemy who must be loved—what then?"

3. Do you have any reflections on Saul's conversion to Paul?

BECOMING WHOLE
AS A SPIRITUAL NECESSITY: A Jungian
Guide to Renewing the Mystic Vision

Individuation and Mysticism: Initiated Knowledge

My purpose in writing and in teaching is to try to present Jung's work in a clear manner. This approach will help transform the mystical path from a medieval to a modern perspective. I've done this in an effort to clarify these paths for people living in our busy world who would like to find a spiritual or psychological orientation that supports a fulfilling life.

Our desire to have answers to the questions that the theologian Martin Buber articulated—"Can you teach me to have faith in reality, in the truth of our existence, so that my life will have purpose, meaning, and a way of being fulfilled?"—comes from a mysterious source within us. We can cope with life, manage our affairs, and be successful in a conventional sense. And yet this mysterious longing will persist. The uncertainty of life is also a mystery. Longing and uncertainty keep us on the edge—keep us awake, alive, aware—and urge us to pay greater attention to who we are and how we are living. The mystical path and individuation, Jung's word for our journey into wholeness, give us a process for embracing the mystery and the uncertainty and for, as I say in my book *Sacred Selfishness* (p. 53), turning "our crises into epiphanies, our struggles into inner teachers, and our mistakes into potentials for change that all lead to a more complete and satisfying life. It also teaches us to honor our difficulties and realize that our

121

ability to experience joy is measured by our willingness to search for meaning in our suffering."

There are still some people who ask me why we should go to all of this trouble. What are the promises of individuation or a spiritual life anyway? I believe the paths promise the following: (1) The life you live will be your own—an authentic life. (2) Such a life is always an adventure. (3) As C. S. Lewis pointed out, such a life is glorious—it is beyond our imagination. (4) In this kind of life, suffering has meaning. (5) Every day is an experience of a piece of eternity. (6) And, finally, we learn how life is love.

But let me be honest at this point, I have never known anyone who chose this path because of its benefits. We are chosen for it. And our awakening—the crack in the illusion of how we are living, which gives rise our call—generally comes in the form of a personal crisis.

Metamorphosis

I want to be clear on a few points as we begin. Individuation and spiritual development are not about self-improvement. Self-improvement is like fixing up an old house: putting on a new coat of paint, replacing boards that have dry rot, or remodeling old rooms; or it's like firming-up, losing weight, having more-positive thoughts, and so on. Individuation and spiritual development from the mystical perspective are about transformation. Individuation means a lifetime of full-fledged metamorphosis, analogous to a caterpillar becoming a butterfly again and again. It is learning how to let go of the defining characteristics that once made up our identity, for the sake of becoming something new, something further enhanced by the Divine within us.

And individuation and spiritual growth are not self-actualization. The mythologist Joseph Campbell noted that self-actualization is for people who don't have anything better to live for—people who don't know their personal myth or spiritual purpose in life. Survival, security, prestige, self-development, and even personal relationships are not the primary values a mystically or spiritually inspired person lives for. When one has become awakened to and has experienced the awe of the Divine mystery, and how it wants to live through us, we begin to

122

understand the meaning of the clue Christ gives us when he says, "He that loseth his life for my sake shall find it."

Yet when we begin this path, we may feel like we are becoming self-absorbed. Certainly people close to us who fear our change will accuse us of becoming selfish and irresponsible. However, once we have become experienced in this field, we realize that most of us carry our responsibilities in a very selfish way—as a burden, a weight, an obstacle, or a defense against self-confrontation—which diminishes us and makes us resentful of those for whom we feel responsible.

To find the roots of our responsibilities and obligations, we must journey into the depths of our abilities and how we learned to define our lives, into the very core sense of ourselves. This journey is necessary because we aren't naturally able to perceive reality as it actually is. Generally, what we "see" is shaped by our impressions, history, baggage, and preconceptions. We don't see people as they really are, because we are too busy reacting to the internal experiences they evoke in us. In other words, our vision is clouded by our psychological complexes and shadows. The mystics realized that we need to undergo a methodical system of purification in order to see reality. In psychological language, this means we must bring our dominant personal and cultural complexes out of our shadow, make them conscious, and work our way free of them. It also follows that once we see reality, our way is usually clear, at least for the moment.

Our psychological and spiritual development is always progressive if we are committed to it, though it may not always seem that way—a point we will explore later. This fact means that wisdom, compassion, and love are achieved states—the results of self-knowledge and consciousness. The true seeker, in any of the great traditions, follows a path of methodical discipline that I prefer to call committed discipleship, which results in *initiated knowledge*.

Purification, or in psychological terms, getting to know our shadows, is necessary before we can truly love. The fact is, "We can't love someone we don't really know, especially ourselves." If we don't know ourselves, we can only objectify ourselves. We make ourselves an object and our love is sentimental and/or a fantasy. The same is true as we

We do not Know the others Create distance.

objectify other people and even the Divine. Once the sentimentality fails and the illusion cracks, there is no substance for love to exist on. Love must be subject to subject, known to known, or "I and Thou," as Martin Buber describes it.

If we fail to know ourselves, we have lost the power to know the generative force of love that is reflected in Dante's vision of the "love which moves the sun and other stars." The reality of love, according to Jung and Thomas Merton, is judged by its power to help us get beyond ourselves and to renew ourselves in transcending our present limitations. The function of love is to build the kingdom of unity and peace on this earth and to bring wholeness or holiness to each of us. Love in this sense has little to do with enjoyment and a shallow peace. It is a death and a rebirth through a methodical process of losing the old way of life and identity and being transformed into a larger version of ourselves that is living in a relationship to the Divine within us. Once the Divine is met within, it becomes apparent everywhere. In Jungian psychology, to be in relationship to the Self, our center, will bring us into relationship with the *"anima mundi"*—the Jungian term for the world soul. Merton suggests, "All true love is therefore associated with three fundamentally human strivings: with creative work, with sacrifice, and with contemplation."

Questions to Expand Our Understanding

Now I would like to ask you to make purification more personal.

1. Make a list of general beliefs that have structured your life.
2. As you did this, what kinds of feelings came up in you?
3. Were you surprised?

Exploring the Illusions

There are two reasons I think it is important to explore the illusions we developed growing up. First, these illusions guided the formation of our personality, which we need in order to be strong and able to function in the world; and our personality provides the foundation for both individuation and the mystical journey. And secondly, we have to become aware that however strong and successful our personality initially is, it really isn't authentic on the personal level.

The mystics defined a person with a strong personality, with the potential for spiritual development, as a *Green Lion*, a symbolic term that is used in spiritual alchemy. Green signifies that the person is spiritually undeveloped. The image of the lion shows the person has the strength and vitality to live successfully on the material level. In symbolic language, the mystics think that humanity in its strength is slain to the world, passes through the mystic death, and is resurrected in a transformed state, that of the Red Dragon. The Red Dragon is the symbol of the free spiritual life that is as powerful on the material level as it is on the spiritual level. The dragon is powerful on the earth and in the sky.

When I share my story in my books, you see that I was a successful man—I was married, had three children, and owned twelve stores in Atlanta. And even though I was depressed and my life was collapsing, if you had asked me about the status of my life, I would have replied that I was a unique individual living a creative destiny. If you had asked me if I loved myself, I would have looked at you kind of funny for asking such an odd question, and I would have answered, "Of course."

The fact is that I was living a pattern designed collectively by society, friends, church, job, and traditions. The only thing unique about it was how my childhood wounds and successes operated to shape the living of this pattern. And I didn't have a clue about what loving myself meant or that you can't love somebody you don't really know. I was a Green Lion; my depression and restlessness were my call to awaken.

The Mystic Way and Individuation

Now I am going to talk more about the Mystic Way and Individuation and look again at Evelyn Underhill's Eight Stages of Mystical Growth. In her landmark study, *Mysticism: The Nature and Development of Spiritual Consciousness*, Underhill sets out to describe the process of a mystic way common to those people who grow into a direct relationship with the Divine. She concludes that all of us who seek meaning in our lives are kindred spirits to the mystics. In Chapter 5, I outlined some of her definitions of the Eight Stages of Mystical Growth and their psychological equivalents. I mentioned that Underhill uses a lower case *r* as the symbol of our busy, everyday reality. In psychological terms this is the reality of the ego; the world of Jung's number one personality, which he described in his autobiography, *Memories, Dreams, Reflections*. Underhill uses a capital *R* to symbolize Eternal Reality, from which the mystery and life force pour into our world and experience. In Jungian psychology, this capital *R* Reality is the world of the collective unconscious and the Self, where the Self may be described as the divine spark that the mystics see in each of us, that gives us our life force and the feeling of life's mystery, and that contains the unique pattern and potential for our lives. In *Memories, Dreams, Reflections*, Jung connected his number two personality to this aspect. Let's now review Underhill's Eight Stages of Mystical Growth.

Stage 1: Awakening

You become aware in some way that the world isn't what you thought it was and you are not who you thought you were. A disturbance of personal equilibrium brings an awareness of a larger world no longer under control, and that leaves one feeling small, like a child. There is the beginning of the realization of the twofold nature of the Divine—it is both being and becoming. Because of our society's distance from spiritual understanding, our calls to awaken often come as personal crises, emotional and physical symptoms, mistakes, and difficulties that threaten our equilibrium and feelings of safety and direction. Thus we are called to seek help.

Awakening is a shock because it leaves us with the knowledge that "getting back to normal" will put us on the same path that made us sick or unhappy to begin with. This realization introduces us to the stage the mystics call purification. (Note: Part 1 in my book *Sacred Selfishness* discusses awakening.)

Stage 2: Purification

The second stage requires practices that help one reclaim a relationship with the interior life. Purification demands commitment and intentional activity with the goal of ridding oneself of the veils and illusions of the unexamined life. Spiritual practices focus on a release from the old ways and illusions. This stage calls for heroic passions in the soul. Jungian psychology or analysis can be a similar process of self-examination and seeking self-knowledge that will continue through all of the stages; during purification we seek to identify wounds, attitudes, and other influences that have driven our life, creating the illusions of our perceptions and the ideas of who we are.

As difficult as purification is, it is the journey that enlarges who we are and leads to the rewards of illumination. (Part 1 and part 2 in *Sacred Selfishness* deal with purification from a psychological standpoint.)

Stage 3: Illumination

Here, one begins to see the beauty and patterns in life. Life intensifies; perception is exalted; feelings of suffering, joy, and love become clear experience. Intuition and an appreciation for the transcendent aspects of life grow. One lives in two worlds, with vocation in reality but with a steady relationship with the Divine. Psychologically, we continue the journey into individual consciousness and the pursuit of self-knowledge.

Emphasis is on getting to know the shadow—the various parts of oneself and how to relate to them and apprehend a pattern in one's life while also becoming grounded in one's humanity. Practices such as befriending dreams, journaling, and active imagination become increasingly important.

Illumination opens us to the knowledge of how to live what Jung called the symbolic life. (Part 2 in *Sacred Selfishness* offers guidance and explanations for this work.)

Stage 4: Voices and Visions

One sees, hears, and interacts with a larger Reality. This includes dreams and visions for the mystic. One sees and hears with more than the five senses, and this is a state of revealing and interacting with a much larger Reality. Psychologically, dream work and active imagination become more important. Archetypal patterns—particularly shadow, anima, and animus—are revealed. Intuition intensifies. One is well into the

THE SEARCH FOR SELF AND THE SEARCH FOR GOD

stage of individual consciousness and is aware of the Self and its energy. (Part 2 in *Sacred Selfishness* continues its guidance in this area.)

These first four stages lead us to a deeper appreciation of and need for periods of contemplation in our lives.

Stage 5: Introversion

Quietness, silence, and prayer become the mainstay of the mystical life and a refuge and a place of renewal from the busy world of reality. Quietness opens one to the journey to the center and requires a new refusal of the values of ordinary reality. There is a renewed openness to rapture and joy as one finds the resources of the center.

Psychologically, inner work is seen as pleasure, renewal, and the ground of one's continued growth. It brings contentment as well as relief, comfort, and direction when times are troubling. Inner work also brings the assurance we are part of something bigger that supports us—that is, the ego is supported by the unconscious and the Self. (Part 2 of *Sacred Selfishness* continues to support this aspect of the journey.) The experience of coming home to ourselves and feeling at home in the world leads to the next stage.

Stage 6: Ecstasy and Rapture

For the mystics, this stage is about the art and science of happiness, the openness to love, a feeling of union with the Divine, and the knowledge that spiritual storms enhance vitality. In the past this stage was often experienced physically as a trance state. Emotionally, it is a feeling of unity and enhanced perception. Psychologically, one has reached the point in individual consciousness where one feels at home in oneself and life. Self-knowledge is bringing balance to living. Love and other relationships no longer reflect illusions, needy psychological pursuits, or idealistic fantasies, nor does one's self-image.

One has learned self-forgiveness and self-love as a foundation for loving others and life. Interestingly, this stage is followed by a new plunge into the chaos of transformation, which is the next stage. (Part 2 in *Sacred Selfishness*, especially chapter 10, helps us understand that inner work must be a work of love.)

128

Stage 7: The Dark Night of the Soul

This is the time of further destruction and construction in one's interior. It is the mystic death of an old state of consciousness and the birth of a new one. This stage requires surrender, and suffering tests one's love when God, or the Divine, seems to have disappeared and everything goes wrong. Saint John of the Cross calls this a time of holy darkness because it marks a major turning point in our perception of Reality and the Divine.

Psychologically, this is a time when we realize that growth and individuation aren't what we thought they were. Joy disappears. One faces the remaining specters of old forms, habits, attitudes, and emotional problems again as further preparation for growth. The ego is being put through the stage of transformation from "I want" and "I should" to "I serve" the Self, or the Divine within, on a more profound level. (Part 3 in *Sacred Selfishness* begins to show how we may experience this stage in relationships and in facing basic wounds.)

Stage 8: The Unitive Life

The next stage or level on this spiral staircase is known as the unitive life. For the mystic there is a unification of the personality on a higher level. Knowledge, will, and love are joined and satisfied and serve the Divine. Life is filled with a transcendent vitality and heroic activity. Being and becoming are joined. There is a marriage of the Soul and the Divine.

Psychologically, this state is reflected in the stage of illuminated consciousness, which is the realization of our unique personalities and their relationships to our deeper Selves and all life. The ego is able to live in relationship and service to the Self. The search for self-knowledge is a natural choice in life, as is growth.

The person has become a person of "substance," who loves life and gives energy, vitality, and hope to the people around him or her. This does not mean there are no more challenges. It means we recognize the stages, often reluctantly, when we have to face them anew—for life is always a challenge to create a larger version of ourselves when on the mystical path.

Questions to Expand Our Understanding

Now let me ask you a few questions to stimulate your reflections:

1. Does the parallel between the process of spiritual growth and individuation now seem clear to you?

2. Did any part surprise you?

3. How did you feel when you read the material about stage 5, introversion, which said that inner work becomes a pleasure and brings renewal and contentment?

To have the work no longer oriented toward problem solving and crisis resolution, but toward discovery and transformation, is often a difficult turning point for clients, therapists, and spiritual directors, because it goes against the grain of our culture. As we continue, there are several major points in this process that I think we need to keep in mind. The first one is that Underhill, like Jung, believes the search for self-knowledge is the one indispensable task in developing spiritual consciousness.

Then we must keep in mind that self-examination is difficult because it opens our eyes to the fact that the world is not what we think it is, we are not who we think we are, and our values are one-sided and insufficient for sustaining a fulfilling life. Plus, events initially force us into self-examination in most cases.

Questions for Reflection   *to maintain our illusions*

Now let me ask you to go back to my statement that "to have the work no longer oriented toward problem solving and crisis resolution, but toward discovery and transformation, is often a difficult turning point for clients, therapists, and spiritual directors."

1. Can you think of some reasons why this statement is true?

2. What are your thoughts and feelings about the obstacles we face as we reach this turning point?

The next thing I try to keep in mind is that the process of purification hurts. We've just heard something about that in our examples. Ex-

130

amining my life destroyed my illusion of childhood and led me to see the moments when I was bruised, scared, and shamed and even traumatized. It forced me to see where my parents failed me, as well as where my Sunday school image of God shattered during the anguish of my mother's death. Looking inward opened the chest where I had carefully packed my childhood—which I thought I could simply store in the basement.

But there was also another side to this process because the pain was cleansing. It opened my eyes to reality and freed me from the sometimes happy and sometimes tragic fable I had concocted about my early life and the people in it. You can begin to see that to some extent, this process is already one of passion, suffering, and transformation.

Questions to Expand Our Understanding

1. In considering what I have just said, describe your thoughts and feelings about this statement: "If one is unwilling to take on the challenge of engagement with the larger Self, then we experience the truth of Jung's observation that service to our neurosis becomes our unconscious religion."

2. What are some of your ideas about how this can happen in our lives?

3. How can the unwillingness to engage our larger Self affect our bodies?

Continuing the Work

As the first stage of our inner work is ending, we are faced with two questions: (1) Who am I outside of the roles I've uncovered? (2) Who will I become? Whether these questions are considered a matter for psychology or religion is simply not important. It is in the process of searching for the answer to them that a healthier and more fulfilling life emerges. However, I'll mention that this search moves us into the psychological stage of individual consciousness and the next stage of the mystical journey: the illuminative way.

The mystics developed a set of spiritual practices or exercises, like those of Saint Ignatius of Loyola, to guide their development into spiritual consciousness. As I think I make it clear in my book, my spiritual practices, in addition to going to analysis and reading, are journaling, dream work, and active imagination.

Journaling, as a form of reflection that I describe, is still the foundation of my transformation. These reflections and listening to dreams keep me in touch with the inner voice that has moved me to view my life in new ways. Active imagination, Jung's technique for interacting consciously with inner aspects of ourselves, is another life-enriching, life-changing practice I use. These practices become a deep conversation with myself, a way of getting to know myself, that leads me into a deep conversation with the Divine and then back into the world as a life-giver.

Questions for Reflection

1. What are some of the practices that you use to stay in touch with the inner voice? (I've heard a range of surprising answers: dance, yoga, fly-fishing, vacuuming, etc.)

2. Has journaling become part of your practice?

Facing the Shadow and Finding a Transformed Life

After I've mentioned a few reflections, I'm going share a short story with you. This is a story that you may recognize. It's about how we split ourselves and about the Divine nature of reconciliation or becoming more whole. In fact, this story may show us how we have split our potential Green Lion out of our personality. Our social and even our religious personae do a good job of helping us define ourselves along the lines of shallow ideals that may put our lion in a cage. Many of you are aware that we build our shadows as we build our identities.

In *Sacred Selfishness* (p. 244), I say, "They're like two sides of the same coin. Every time we identify with a value such as 'It's good to be active and efficient' we reject its opposite—it's as if we've said, 'It's bad to be lazy and lackadaisical.' Eventually our identities are based on collections of such identifications and they define who we believe we are." Much of our shadow cannot be transformed. But much can. Many of us were taught to repress our aggression, our anger, our fierceness, our sensuality, and our capacity to desire. We were even taught to label these things as all that is brutal, vile, and vicious in

132

the human character. Yet many of these things can be of great value when they become known and under conscious control. What can't be transformed cannot be ignored either or we will not know how to deal with it. To learn about our shadow is the difference between being naïve and being wise. Such wisdom gives us the strength to stand for and engender life.

Without this wisdom we will unconsciously negate life, even when we do our best to perform good works. Understanding these realities explains why we need to stay away from people who think they are saints or even good and faithful. However, observing the development, the struggle, and conflict involved in becoming a real saint can help us see the parallel between spiritual development and individuation.

Now I will invite you to sit back and relax and see what happens to a future saint when he meets the most reviled part of himself on the road.

Giovanni Francesco di Bernardone is born to become a wealthy merchant around the turn of the twelfth century. But other forces are working behind the scenes, shaping his destiny to become Saint Francis of Assisi. Change is in the air in Italy. In the foreground of everyday life, ambition drives the emerging classes of merchants and warriors.

In the background, the power of the church is becoming as oriented toward earthly authority as it is toward heavenly devotion. Life's foreground initially molds our identities, secretly forming us in the image of the social character of our time. Yet beneath the surface of appearances, the spiritual power of the church still affected people and drew many into the need for devotion to a higher purpose in life.

Ambition, conflict, and possibilities greet Giovanni's arrival. His father, Pietro, is a man of the new times. A merchant, a member of the new class that is overthrowing the old division of nobles and serfs, Pietro hard charges into success, pursuing money and power with a dedication that matches our ambitious pursuits today. Foreshadowing the future of modern life, he puts business and commercial affairs ahead of everything else. Pietro is succeeding and pulling his family into what we might call the upper middle class.

Giovanni's mother, Pica, on the other hand is the spiritual opposite of her husband. She is a pious woman, devoted to the church—a woman with a strong spiritual vision for her newborn son. In response to her expectations for her son's life, she names him Giovanni, or John, after John the Baptist. In the middle ages, a child's name was thought to have a strong influence on who he or she would become. Thus, Pica sought to take control of her son's life while Pietro was away on business.

Pietro returns home and is furious at the deception. Unwilling to give in to his wife or give up his own ambitions for Giovanni's future— much less see it modeled after a desert hermit—he adds *Francesco* to his son's name. Because Pietro is making a fortune selling wool and silk in France, he is sure this name will add power to his son's future.

Giovanni—who is to become a man of great simplicity—has a childhood filled with luxury and educational and social activities. Pietro insists on fine schools and the best clothes. As a young man, Giovanni becomes well-known for his parties, which draw young noblemen from near and far. In contrast to his habitual generosity, he hides a darker sensitivity, for he is completely repulsed by anyone who is dirty, poor, or disfigured by disease.

Giovanni is also a dreamer. At school he is enchanted by the stories of knights and their adventures. He sits spellbound at the annual pageant that repeats the story of Saint George rescuing the princess from a terrible dragon. Noble dreams flourish in his young mind, and he develops a secret ambition to be a knight, not a merchant, and to follow the road to adventure.

But his dreams are smashed when his father takes him into his business and follows the medieval custom of initiating him into his trade. By now wealthy and powerful, Pietro envisions his son carrying his name and fortune into the future. And in fact, Giovanni is an expert at making money and is even better at arranging banquets, parties, and dances—given with generosity and elegance. But in the secret recesses of the young man's heart, his dreams of knighthood and glory still remain.

During this period of history, Italy isn't really a country. It is a collection of small states that have a bloody history of feuds, competitiveness, and battling one another over real and even imagined causes. One day the people of Assisi and the aristocrats in Perugia insult and spark each other into a war. The old dreams of knighthood seize Giovanni and he sees his chance for glory. Immediately he rides out to battle, filled with martial enthusiasm, much to his mother's sorrow and his father's chagrin.

The war, however, quickly becomes a disaster that sears the soul of the future saint. The army of Assisi is easily crushed and Giovanni witnesses the terrible slaughter of lifelong friends and neighbors. Giovanni is captured, cast into a foul dungeon, and imprisoned for months. He wastes away, is racked with violent fevers, and suffers intensely in the rat-infested, dank rooms of clammy stone. Finally he is released, probably ransomed by his father.

When he returns to his merchant life, his soul is clearly wounded. Making money loses its savor. Parties leave him hung over and haunted by memories of the grief and desolation he has seen and experienced. His noble dreams of glory have turned to ashes, leaving him filled with an inner restlessness as he faces what seems like a barren future. In desperation, he undertakes a pilgrimage to Rome. But even in the presence of Saint Peter's, he finds the spiritual teachings of his childhood hollow and meaningless.

Soon after returning home, he is riding horseback down the road to the hospital, as usual absorbed in his thoughts. Suddenly the horse jerks to the side of the road. With difficulty Francis pulls the horse back by a violent yank at the reins. The young man looks up and recoils in horror. A leper stands in the middle of the road, a short distance away, unmoving, and looking at him. This leper is no different from the others, the usual wan specter with a stained face, shaved head, dressed in gray sackcloth. He does not speak and shows no sign of moving, of getting out of the way. He looks at the horseman directly, strangely, with an acute and penetrating gaze.

An instant that seems like eternity passes. Slowly Francis dismounts, goes to the man, and takes his hand. It is a poor emaciated hand, bloodstained, twisted, inert, and cold like the hand of a corpse. Francis puts a mite of charity in the hand, presses it, and carries it to his lips. And as he kisses the lacerated flesh of the creature who is the most abject, the most hated, the most scorned of all human beings, he is suddenly flooded with a wave of emotion, one that shuts out everything around him, one that he would remember even on his deathbed. The leper withdraws his hand; Francis raises his head to look at him again. He is no longer there.

The first biographers describe this episode in poetic passages, seeing it as a revelation of the divine. Or perhaps it is a sign that God always works through the broken and reviled. In psychological terms, it may be an opening to all that Francis has rejected within himself.

In any event, after this experience the world changes. Giovanni sees reality in a different way and begins to sense that rather than being a merchant, he can find a more profound place in the creative unfolding of life. In his new state of openness, he goes into an old, decaying church to pray quietly. In the silence he hears a voice from an old painting of Christ on the cross say, "Francis, go and repair my house." The command is repeated three times.

At this point one of his major mistakes leads him into his destiny. Based on his past success as a merchant, he thinks of fundraising in order to repair the church. He rushes back to the family business, takes their best collection of fabrics to the next town, and sells them. Fortunately events catch up with him before he spends the money. His outraged father, furious in his disappointment over the failure his son is becoming, charges him with theft and brings him to trial before the bishop. The trial is in the town square. Pietro pours out his anguish and fury in front of the bishop and the whole town of Assisi.

Following the bishop's instructions, Francis returns the money to his father. As he completes this transaction, he has a vision of Lady Poverty and declares to the whole community that thereafter he will refer to only his Father in Heaven as his father. He then returns everything that he had received from his human father to him, including the clothes on his back. The bishop is so moved by this act that he arises and covers Francis with his own cloak. This marks the end of the first stage in the lifelong journey of transformation made by Saint Francis. (This account is based on the narrative in *Francis of Assisi* by Arnaldo Fortini.)

Questions for Reflection

1. As you are thinking about the story, write down the image or images that affected you the most.

2. Now I would like for you to reflect for a few more minutes and write down the feelings, ideas, and questions the story brought up in you.

3. How did this story remind you of parts of your own unlived life?

Kissing the Leper

The idea of "kissing the leper" is a powerful one in psychology as well as in spirituality. Dr. Jung talked a lot about the teleological aspects of symptoms and the idea that our neuroses or dysfunctions are the signs of a life that hasn't found its meaning. In other words our symptoms and dysfunctions are calling us to transform and become more comprehensive versions of ourselves. In my books, I show how I have people dialogue with their leper. Dialogue comes from two words, *dia* and *logos*, whose definitions suggest "meaning flowing through."

In these exercises, our leper broadens our personality, deepens our humanity, and expands our ability through understanding to have compassion. We have many kinds of symbolic lepers within us. Fear, addictions, compulsions and inner critic as well as physical symptoms such as back pain, depression, and weight problems are examples I give in my writing. It is often hard to see how these things can be transformed into something positive. But they always hide something important to our wholeness, and they may even have the chance to become our spiritual director (or inspiring daimon).

In symbolic terms, a kiss is a transformative act. It is not an embrace. The princess kissed the frog to transform it. She didn't embrace it. The figurative kiss is an act that involves humbling ourselves as well as doing something personal and intimate that acknowledges our leper.

Let me give you an example from real life. I had worked with Trudi for over a year. Trudi is a professional person, also married with children, in her early forties. No matter what issue we worked on, she always came back to how distressed she was about being thirty-five pounds over her normal weight. Of course she had tried Weight Watchers, many diets, cognitive therapy, and exercise. Repeated failures had only made her feel worse about herself.

Finally, I suggested that she dialogue with her weight. She tried and nothing happened. Then I suggested that she dialogue with "Fat Trudi". "Oh, drat," she said, "that might work."

Trudi began her dialogue writing, "Fat Trudi, I hate you, I despise you! You make me look bad! You make me feel bad! You embarrass me! I am ashamed for even my husband to see me. You destroy my self-esteem!"

Fat Trudi replied, "Stop right there! I've had enough of this finger pointing, nagging, and hatred. Do you think I'm in here because I want to be? I'm in here because you created me—you used me. I know how you hate me. You show so much compassion to your kids and others, but none for me. Where is that Divine love you're always going on about?"

Trudi is stunned, taken aback, and writes, "How can I help? I realize how destructive hate is. You are the pain and darkness in my life. You must be carrying my cross."

Fat Trudi replies, "I have never felt love. Acknowledge me. I crave the sweet life. I want to be happy, to get attention and appreciation. I'm the lady at the well that Christ loved. You have to learn how to be passionate about your—or rather, our—life."

Trudi says, "I don't know...I don't know how to love myself. Can you teach me?"

Fat Trudi answers, "I don't know. You always think you're right. Talk to me until we trust each other and I will try. Only a bigger love can turn hatred into love."

This dialogue was written spontaneously. It is only a beginning. But it can help us see how a symbolic approach that sets up a relationship with our most despised aspect can result in "meaning flowing through". Trudi dialogued with Fat Trudi for two years. Somewhere along the way, after about nine months, the weight began to melt away.

Questions to Expand Our Understanding

1. Are there parts of yourself that you secretly feel this way about? How good are any of us at telling ourselves we love or like ourselves when we know down deep something is wrong?

2. To what use can you put the information we've been talking about?

3. Does it give you any insight into our collective consciousness? (We have a tendency to hate parts of ourselves not because they are evil, but because they are shaming.)

Questions For Reflection

1. Consider your early dreams, secret dreams that you once had that may have been fulfilled or destiny forming, like Saint Francis's dream of being a knight. Do you think Francis became a spiritual knight? How?

2. Where do you see the "wasteland" situations in his life? Are they in the traps of responsibility, the traps of dependency, the traps of socially and religiously appropriate behavior?

3. How do you think Saint Francis found what to give his heart to? (Despair is passionate; depression is lukewarm.)

4. To what use can you put these reflections?

The Path of Initiated Knowledge

As we are preparing to discuss self-love and initiated knowledge, let me tell you a little more about myself. I was raised in the Protestant South. And as I said in my lecture, I was taught to be quiet, controlled, polite all of the time—no matter what was happening. I was also taught that good people were loving people, and that meant always forgiving and helping everybody else. In fact, it boiled down in many cases to pleasing everybody else and believing I could put on "goodness" like a clean shirt. I remember one woman who told me, echoing the words of many people I've worked with, that her self-approval was determined by everyone else's approval. Were any of you brought up that way?

The journey out from under these influences and into vocation has taught me the importance of initiated knowledge. This knowledge can come only through the kind of self-confrontation we have been talking about. This kind of knowledge cannot be taught in a traditional education system because it can be acquired only through individual insight and personal experience. We quickly see how necessary living wholeheartedly is for us to have the necessary experience to reflect upon and to develop self-knowledge. And we cannot live a wholehearted life alone.

Quotations for Reflection

In order to help explore self-love and compassion further, read this first paragraph, which is one of my favorite quotes from Underhill's book on mysticism (p. 47), and write your reflections about the quotation.

1. The Green Lion, though few would divine it, is the First Matter of the Great Work: hence, in spiritual alchemy, natural man in his wholeness—Salt, Sulphur, and Mercury in their crude state. He is called green because, seen from the transcendent standpoint, he is still unripe, his latent powers undeveloped; and a Lion because of his strength, fierceness, and virility. Here the common opinion that a pious effeminacy, a diluted and amiable spirituality, is the proper raw material of the mystic life is emphatically contradicted. (It is not by the education of the lamb, but by the hunting and taming of the wild intractable lion, instinct with vitality, full of ardor and courage, exhibiting heroic qualities on the sensual plane, that the Great Work is achieved.) The lives of the saints enforce the same law.

This perspective goes against everything I was taught growing up. Now, take about five minutes to write your reflections about this quotation.

Now let's do the same thing for this second paragraph.

2. Wholehearted engagement with our inner and outer lives gives us the food for our reflections. Jung underlines that we cannot obtain the knowledge beforehand that can come only as a result of being committed to a full engagement in life. To support his point, he relates the story of Saul's conversion to Paul in the same talk to a clergy convention that I mentioned previously. Jung said, "Saul owed his conversion neither to true love, nor to true faith, nor to any other truth. It was solely his hatred of the Christians that set him on the road to Damascus and to that decisive experience which was to alter the whole course of his life. He was brought to this experience by following out, with conviction, his own worst mistake." In another place, Jung used this story to illustrate that if we pursue the wrong thing with all of our heart, we will end up at the right place.

So, now take about five minutes to write your reflections about this quotation.

Now repeat with this third paragraph:

140

3. Jung points out: "Everything good is costly, and the development of personality is one of the most costly of all things. (It is a matter of saying yea to oneself, of taking oneself as the most serious of tasks, of being conscious of everything one does, and keeping it constantly before one's eyes in all its dubious aspects—truly a task that taxes us to the utmost.)" And he continues by saying: "But the Westerner who wishes to set out on this way, if he is really serious about it, has all authority against him—intellectual, moral, and religious."

What are some of the most significant and personal aspects of our conventional wisdom and moral and religious attitudes that have trapped you and been major stumbling blocks in your growth and journey? What else moves you personally in these two statements from Jung?

Now, take about five minutes to write your reflections about this quotation.

And finally, here is the fourth paragraph:

4. Many of us felt trapped, bullied, and shamed by the creeds and doctrines of shallow approaches to religion in institutions we grew up in. What would be your response if you took the position of Karen Armstrong that a creed should mean "what we give our heart to"? What would be some of the ingredients of your credo?

Again, take about five minutes to write your reflections about this quotation.

There are two additional questions that I would like to ask you:

1. What surprised you about this experience?

2. What moved or inspired you the most?

In closing, I would like to say that I think the mystic vision is a vision that considers the Divine a force of love and a force of creativity—the mystic quest is the journey of coming into relationship with these forces or powers. And it is no simple quest, yet it reminds us that we are here to become fully human.

141

Resources

C. G. Jung Resources

Jung, C. G. (1933). Modern man in search of a soul (W. S. Dell & C. F. Baynes, Trans.). New York, NY: Harcourt, Brace and Company.

Jung, C. G. (1954). Studies in word association (R. F. C. Hull, Trans.). In H. Read, M. Fordham, G. Adler, & W. McGuire (Eds.), The Collected Works of C. G. Jung: Vol. 2. Experimental researches. Princeton, NJ: Princeton University Press.

Jung, C. G. (1954). H. Read, M. Fordham, G. Adler, & W. McGuire (Eds.), The Collected Works of C. G. Jung: Vol. 5. Symbols of transformation (R. F. C. Hull, Trans.). Princeton, NJ: Princeton University Press.

Jung, C. G. (1954). The relations between the ego and the unconscious (R. F. C. Hull, Trans.). In H. Read, M. Fordham, G. Adler, & W. McGuire (Eds.), The Collected Works of C. G. Jung: Vol. 7. Two essays on analytical psychology. Princeton, NJ: Princeton University Press.

Jung, C. G. (1954). H. Read, M. Fordham, G. Adler, & W. McGuire (Eds.), The Collected Works of C. G. Jung: Vol. 8: The structure and dynamics of the psyche (R. F. C. Hull, Trans.). Princeton, NJ: Princeton University Press.

Jung, C. G. (1954). Psychological aspects of the mother archetype (R. F. C. Hull, Trans.). In H. Read, M. Fordham, G. Adler, & W. McGuire (Eds.), The Collected Works of C. G. Jung: Vol. 9, Pt. 1. The archetypes and the collective unconscious. Princeton, NJ: Princeton University Press.

Jung, C. G. (1954). H. Read, M. Fordham, G. Adler, & W. McGuire (Eds.), The Collected Works of C. G. Jung: Vol. 10. Civilization in transition (R. F. C. Hull, Trans.). Princeton, NJ: Princeton University Press.

Jung, C. G. (1954). H. Read, M. Fordham, G. Adler, & W. McGuire (Eds.), The Collected Works of C. G. Jung: Vol. 11. Psychology and religion: West and East (R. F. C. Hull, Trans.). Princeton, NJ: Princeton University Press.

Jung, C. G. (1954). Commentary on The Secret of the Golden Flower (R. F. C. Hull, Trans.). In H. Read, M. Fordham, G. Adler, & W. McGuire (Eds.), The Collected Works of C. G. Jung: Vol. 13. Alchemical studies. Princeton, NJ: Princeton University Press.

Jung, C. G. (1954). Rex and Regina (R. F. C. Hull, Trans.). In H. Read, M.

Fordham, G. Adler, & W. McGuire (Eds.), The Collected Works of C. G. Jung: Vol. 14. Mysterium coniunctionis. Princeton, NJ: Princeton University Press.

Jung, C. G. (1954). H. Read, M. Fordham, G. Adler, & W. McGuire (Eds.), The Collected Works of C. G. Jung: Vol. 18. The symbolic life (R. F. C. Hull, Trans.). Princeton, NJ: Princeton University Press.

Jung, C. G. (1961). A. Jaffé (Ed.), Memories, dreams, reflections. New York: NY: Vintage.

Jung, C. G. (Ed.). (1964). Man and his symbols. New York, NY: Doubleday.

Jung, C. G., Jaffé, A. (in collaboration with). (1976) G. Adler (Ed.), (R. F. C. Hull, Trans.) C. G. Jung Letters: Vols. 1 & 2. London, England: Routledge and Kegan.

Jung, C. G. (1988). Nietzsche's Zarathustra: Notes of the seminar given in 1934–1939. Princeton, NJ: Princeton University Press.

General Resources

Campbell, J. (1968). The hero with a thousand faces. New York, NY: Princeton.

Campbell, J. (Ed.). (1968). The mystic vision: Papers from the Eranos Yearbooks. Princeton, NJ: Princeton University Press.

Campbell, J. (1990). Transformation of myth through time. New York, NY: Harper & Row.

Castillejo, I. C., de. (1973). Knowing woman. New York, NY: Putnam.

Davies, R. (1996). The merry heart: Reflections on reading, writing and the world of books. New York, NY: Penguin.

Dieckmann, H. (1999). Complexes: Diagnosis and therapy in analytical psychology (B. Mathews, Trans.). Evanston, IL: Chiron.

Edinger, E. (1972). Ego and archetype. New York, NY: Penguin Books.

Edinger, E. (1984). The creation of consciousness: Jung's myth for modern man. Toronto, Canada: Inner City.

Eliade, M. (1958). Rites and symbols of initiation. New York, NY: Harper & Row, Torch Books.

Eliade, M. (1987). Encyclopedia of religion. New York, NY: MacMillan.

Franz, M.-L., von. (1978). An introduction to the psychology of fairy tales (4th ed.). Dallas, TX: Spring.

Fromm, E. (1995). R. Funk (Ed.).The essential Fromm: Life between having and being. New York, NY: Continuum.

Harris, B. (2002). Sacred selfishness: A guide to living a life of substance. San Francisco, CA: New World Library.

Harris, B. (2007). The fire and the rose: The wedding of spirituality and sexuality. Evanston, IL: Chiron.

Hillman, J. (1967). Insearch: Psychology and religion. Dallas, TX: Spring Publications.

Huxley, A. The perennial philosophy: An interpretation of the great mystics, East and West. New York, NY: Harper Collins.

Jacobi, J. (1971). Complex/archetype/symbol. New York, NY: Bollingen.

Jaffe, A. (1984). The myth of meaning in the work of C. G. Jung. Zurich, Switzerland: Daimon.

Johnson, R. A. (1986). Inner work: Using dreams and active imagination for personal growth. San Francisco, CA: Harper & Row.

Kast, V. (1977). Father/daughter, mother/son. Rockport, MA: Elements.

Lewis, T., Amin, F., Lannon, R. (2000). A general theory of love. New York, NY: Vintage.

Luke, H. M. (1988). The voice within: Love and virtue in the age of the spirit. New York, NY: Crossroads.

Mattoon, M. (1981). Jungian psychology in perspective. New York, NY: The Free Press.

Neumann, E. (1944). The origins and history of consciousness (R. Mannheim, Trans.). New York, NY: Pantheon.

Neumann, N. (1989). The place of creation. Princeton, NJ: Princeton University Press.

Paz, O. (1990). The other voice: Essays on modern poetry (H. Lane, Trans.). New York, NY: Harcourt.

Rilke, R. M. (1975). Rilke on love and other difficulties (J. J. L. Mood, Trans.). New York, NY: Norton.

Rilke, R. M. (1984). Letters to a young poet (S. Mitchell, Trans.). New York, NY: Random House.

Shalit, E. (2002). The complex: Path of transformation from archetype to ego. Toronto, Canada: Inner City.

Shalit, E. (2008). Enemy, cripple and beggar: Shadows in the hero's path. San Francisco, CA: Fisher King.

Underhill, E. (1999). Mysticism: The nature and development of spiritual consciousness. Oxford, England: One World Publications.

Whitmont, E. G. (1969). The symbolic quest: Basic concepts of analytical psychology. Princeton, NJ: Princeton University Press.

Woodman, M., Danson, K., Hamilton, M., & Allen, R. (1992). Leaving my father's house: A journey to conscious femininity. Boston, MA: Shambala.

Author's Bio

Bud Harris, Ph.D., originally became a businessman and successfully owned his own business before returning to school to become a psychotherapist. After earning his Ph.D. in psychology and practicing as a psychotherapist and psychologist, he experienced the call to further his growth and become a Jungian analyst. He then moved to Zürich, Switzerland where he trained for over five years and graduated from the C. G. Jung Institute. He is the author of ten books, lectures widely, and practices as a Jungian analyst in Asheville, North Carolina.

For additional information about his practice and his work, visit: www.budharris.com.